DATA SCIENCE FOR EXECUTIVES

DATA
SCIENCE
for
EXECUTIVES

Leveraging Machine Intelligence
to Drive Business ROI

NIR KALDERO

LIONCREST
PUBLISHING

DATA SCIENCE FOR EXECUTIVES

Leveraging Machine Intelligence to Drive Business ROI

ISBN   978-1-5445-1269-3 *Hardcover*

      978-1-5445-1125-2 *Paperback*

      978-1-5445-1124-5 *Ebook*

      978-1-5445-1126-9 *Audiobook*

CONTENTS

ACKNOWLEDGMENTS

I dedicate this book to my beloved grandparents, Varda and Jacob, who continue to give me unbounded opportunities to explore, learn, and strive in life. I certainly wouldn't be the man I am today without your support, dedication, guidance, and love. I truly hope this book and its contents will give you so much joy and pride.

A special thank you to Tom Lane, who contributed his editorial skills throughout the writing of this book; my friends and colleagues Dr. Donatella Taurasi and Greg Kamradt for their feedback and support; and the team at Scribe Media, especially Ted Flanagan and Zach Obront.

This book would not have been possible without the contributions of and collaborations and interactions with colleagues, business clients, and peers.

It's my hope that this book will serve as a guide to all of you, as this was the primary reason I embarked on the writing journey.

INTRODUCTION

We are in the Fourth Industrial Revolution, sparked by machine or artificial intelligence (AI). If you are a business leader, you need to ensure your organization's survival. Machine intelligence is having an unprecedented impact on business innovation, and its immediate adoption is the only path to corporate survival.

AI is no longer a futuristic fantasy or chapter in a computer-science textbook. Now is the time for leaders of companies of all sizes to learn how to employ AI to solve the most critical problems we face in our businesses, economy, society, and environment.

We are living in a new era of wealth of data, and we no longer have the capacity to absorb, much less process, it all. We now need to rely on tools and technologies to extend our intelligence, enabling all this data to be processed in an unbiased fashion to help us make better, smarter decisions. I believe we are now in what I call the human + machine era: both/and rather than either/or. We will continue to make our own decisions, but these will and must be assisted by the power of technology.

While many debates and concerns have arisen regarding the purpose of AI and its supposed threat to mankind, I feel it's critical to set the stage with a different message. The purpose of machine intelligence and smart learning systems is to augment—not replace—human intelligence and judgment.

Each and every day, working closely with the world's largest leading technology companies, I see that this technology's purpose is to enhance human capability and potential. I believe that AI should and will make all of us better at our jobs and that its benefits will extend to the many, not just the elite few, across all dimensions of our personal and professional lives.

Although computer scientists have been talking about AI for more than sixty years, machine intelligence is now a reality already transforming many businesses. Incumbent corporations must act now, at this crucial time, to understand how to adopt data science and machine learning techniques to radically transform their businesses, especially by looking at what early adopters of this technology have done: where and how they invested, how they measured their ROI, and how they refined their strategies.

Ten or fifteen years ago, these early adopters started thinking about how they could improve their operations and product development, as well as enhance their user and client experiences and journeys, through machine-intelligence modeling techniques. Innovative, data-driven companies like Google, Facebook, Amazon, and Apple now apply data science and machine intelligence in every part of their businesses. The ROI has been impressive: more than 35 percent increase in revenue and business outcomes.[1] And this is just the beginning.

Machine intelligence is now set to transform the way business is done in large legacy or incumbent companies. Only data- and model-driven companies are likely to survive in the fast-paced climate of the Fourth Industrial Revolution. Looking back, the First Industrial Revolution was about steam and railroads, the Second about electricity, and the Third brought about by the Internet. AI, the basis of the Fourth Industrial Revolution, will completely change the way business is done and companies are run in the next five to ten years, just as the Internet has done in the last ten. The transformation will be bigger than that

1   InfoSys, "AI Adoption Driving Revenue Growth for Businesses; Leadership on Workforce Implications Vital - Infosys Study," press release, January 17, 2017, https://www.infosys.com/newsroom/press-releases/Pages/leadership-workforce-implications-vital.aspx.

any previous revolution has brought about. To compete in the new landscape of the Fourth Industrial Revolution, organizations will be required to drive value by leveraging the vast amount of data they already possess with sophisticated machine-intelligence modeling techniques.

The Internet's Third Industrial Revolution opened the floodgates of connectivity and dramatically increased business globalization through a tremendous influx of data. Enterprises acquire vast amounts of data and will continue to do so every single day. They need to learn how to use machine intelligence technology and tools to capitalize on and leverage this greatly increased data flow, finding the gold nuggets and gemstones still hidden within all this information.

We are in an important time in history. Legacy enterprises must act *now* to transform themselves into data- and model-driven organizations before it is too late. The competition is growing rapidly, and companies that hesitate to change will see their market share eaten up. These are large businesses—including Fortune 25 companies and their international equivalents—so the transformation is going to take a few years. There is no doubt about their ability to transform, but they must act quickly during this crucial period.

While many people in the industry call the Fourth Industrial Revolution the Artificial Intelligence Revolution, I prefer to call it the Machine Intelligence Revolution. We are in an era, especially with respect to research, where we seek to expand our computational power and ability to enhance the "intelligence" of our machines and models. There's a fine line between the terms "machine intelligence," "machine learning," "data science," and "AI." However, "machine intelligence" is both a more realistic and modest term than AI. Human intelligence hasn't yet been imitated artificially, and there's a lot we still don't know about the nature of human intelligence itself. However, machine intelligence and its business applications are already a reality, using sophisticated modeling techniques to process, analyze, and make predictions based on the data businesses already have and will continue to collect at ever-increasing speed.

Also, frankly, many executives find the term AI intimidating. During my "data science for executives" trainings worldwide, attendees are often put off when they are shown, for instance, images of robots in Japanese airports or emotional-intelligence robots such as Pepper. This head-in-the-sand attitude is a real problem since top management needs to embrace and understand, not fear and avoid, the machine intelligence revolution if their companies are to survive and thrive. You must both learn about and seize the opportunities that machine intelligence has opened up.

The truth is that large companies are ready to start leveraging machine intelligence, although the journey will be a long and intimidating one, given these enterprises' sheer size. Embracing the Fourth Industrial Revolution involves cultural transformation, which is no small matter in companies that employ between 60,000 and 2.3 million people worldwide.

These companies have the data and resources to make this transformation, but their top executives and mid-tier management don't yet know how to operationalize the process: what tools they need and what playbook or strategy they should be following. This book will remedy that. Most executives and business leaders have heard a lot about machine learning and data science, but they still don't know what this means in practical terms: how to prioritize their investments and build an environment where this initiative and their people can thrive. They need clear and actionable explanations.

Executives are responsible for keeping their companies competitive. This book will provide the guidelines you need in the Fourth Industrial Revolution: the steps you should take as well as the habits and mindset you should develop to transform your businesses into data- and model-driven organizations.

This book will be useful to all current and prospective

business leaders, no matter what the size of their businesses may be. It also particularly addresses top-level executives and business leaders at large corporations because data science and machine intelligence are top-down initiatives. This transformation requires significant funding, large-scale cultural and operational change, and senior-management leadership. All this must come from the top.

In many organizations, lower-level technical employees are often charged with trying to make and lead this change. These are usually very capable people who want to move their companies into the data-science revolution. They are certainly able to create machine-intelligence models, but they don't have the necessary funding or an executive sponsor ready and able to help them operationalize data science throughout the organization. The business processes and the cultural change required to make this happen are just not there.

Data science, therefore, must start as a top-down initiative. The business leaders and executives responsible for setting strategy, bringing money to the table, and making cultural transformation happen must understand and support the initiative. If the CEO or other C-level executives do not champion data, how can the people below them do so?

By being a granular as possible, this book will help

executives and business leaders overcome the cultural problems of turning their companies into data- and model-driven organizations. At private, closed-door workshops and offsites, I'm always the second speaker in line after McKinsey, Deloitte, Boston Consulting Group, or another major consultancy firm. The first thing I say to the executives present is, "OK, you heard all that. That was a very important, macro-level approach to the problem. Now, let me be granular and specific with you and give you tips, habits, and tools. Let me share my experience working with other large corporations. How can you start transforming your organizations? What you can do today, tomorrow, or right after you leave my workshop? I want you to leave this room (or finish reading this book) with immediate action items."

This book will help executives, business leaders, and business people in general attain greater data literacy and understand this fast-changing field and its jargon. Can you explain in plain English what machine learning is and how it can transform your organization? Most top-level executives can't.

This book will help you comprehend data-science terminology so you can communicate with your technical as well as non-technical teams, develop critical thinking, and be able to judge whether a machine-intelligence project is headed in the right direction. Non-technical executives and technical people need to work together to fully operationalize and deploy machine-intelligence within the enterprise. You need to be able to communicate seamlessly and efficiently with technical people and know enough about data science to understand and critique the results of machine-intelligence modeling and the predictions that land on your desk. You don't need a thorough education in or a grasp of the technology, but you do need to know how to evaluate, think independently, and communicate what's important.

You must be able to translate your top business problems into solvable data and modeling problems so you can set a machine-learning strategy and ensure that all the effort you are investing in data science is aligned with your organization's top business goals. To do this, you need to figure out how to set goals and create metrics that are clear to your technical team, enabling them to develop the right approaches to the right business problems. That's this book's first goal. The second is to help you develop a machine-intelligence mindset, an intuition of when a technical approach will solve a business problem.

No, not all business problems can be solved by leveraging data and modeling techniques. However, in my workshops, when I ask executives to write down their top business problems and identify how many could be solved with data-modeling techniques, the answer they give is usually 75 percent. I believe the figure is actually higher.

This book is divided into three parts. The first covers the principles of data science and transforming your business into a data-driven organization. The second takes you on a step-by-step journey through the data-science workflow. The third consists of case studies, four cutting-edge examples showing how industry leaders have or could leverage machine intelligence to solve their most pressing business problems.

The second part is a general guide to data-science workflow, and the case studies will then walk you through that workflow in a variety of specific situations, showing what questions need to be asked to understand and critique machine-intelligence outcomes and recommendations. The purpose of the case studies is to jump-start thinking about how you could apply machine intelligence in your own enterprise in ways that will yield high ROI.

As you can no doubt already tell, I'm a machine-intelligence enthusiast. In the past five years, I have trained many C-level executives at Fortune 100 and 200 companies, and their international equivalents—which have operated successfully for decades, employed thousands of people, and generated billions of dollars every year—on how to start the journey of transforming their organizations in the Fourth Industrial Revolution. This book shares what I have learned from teaching and working closely with these business leaders.

My personal mission is to advance the world through education, science, and technology, which is what inspired me to join Galvanize, a cutting-edge technology-education company and learning community. Galvanize has given me a wealth of experience working with the data-science community around the world and with executives in both the private and public sectors.

This is also why I embarked on the journey to write this book. I felt I gained so much experience and knowledge that I couldn't keep it to myself anymore. I want to unleash it to help make the world a better place for many generations to come.

Five years ago, I architected and created Galvanize's Master of Science in Data Science Program, the third ever in the world. The program is built around three unique, innovative pillars. The first is a hands-on approach to theory, in which theoretical problems are always solved in a business context and with real data. The second is immersion: stuents and instructors work closely together inside and outside the classroom. Our third, most innovative approach is the practicum, which links academia with the private and public sectors to give students real working experience while they pursue their education and training.

I am also privileged to be a Google expert and mentor, and an IBM champion, helping the analytics and design communities around the world. I started working in the field when I joined the Israeli military service at age eighteen and leveraged data to increase efficiency and save lives. Although we didn't call what I was doing machine learning or data science back then, I was able to get experience and expertise early on in how to translate business problems into solvable data problems. After completing my service, I studied in Israel and at UC Berkeley, and today my mission is to help the world advance into the new era. To sum up, I'm a data-science expert, educator, and executive who seeks to help business leaders solve their business problems by leveraging and operationalizing machine-intelligence techniques that quickly realize ROI.

If you are ready to rise and meet the challenges of the Fourth Industrial Revolution, this essential guide will enable you to take your business to the next level.

PART I

MACHINE INTELLIGENCE

THE FOURTH INDUSTRIAL REVOLUTION

CHAPTER 1

GETTING SERIOUS ABOUT MACHINE INTELLIGENCE

Machine intelligence—the Fourth Industrial Revolution—is here and now, and the rate at which it is transforming business is unprecedented. Since most industries leverage data to obtain insight into their businesses and customers, we can see this revolution everywhere: in healthcare, e-commerce, energy, government, education, energy, and security, among many other industries. Every business can and will need to benefit from machine intelligence. It is coming fast.

In thinking about how fast things can change, consider this photo:

It's Easter morning in the year 1900, and New York's Fifth Avenue is filled with horse-drawn carriages. There's only one motor car.

Now look at this image:

It's Easter morning 1913, and Fifth Avenue is filled with cars. There is only one horse-drawn carriage in the street. In just thirteen years, the automobile completely changed societies everywhere.

So imagine the accelerating speed of change today, with the Internet, social media, globalization, and machine intelligence. Companies that don't take advantage of today's opportunities will probably not survive the next five years. Time is short, pressing, and crucial.

THE FOURTH INDUSTRIAL REVOLUTION

Computers have long been able to beat grand masters at chess but not master players of the Asian board game Go. AlphaGo's March 2016 victory over world champion Lee Sedol was a major AI milestone. Some experts believed an AI program as powerful as AlphaGo was at least five years in future; others though it would take twice as long.

AlphaGo's algorithms are more general-purpose than the chess algorithms of IBM's Deep Blue and Watson, back in the day. It was now time, many experts believed, to begin discussing the potential impact of machines with general-purpose intelligence.

AlphaGo's algorithms weren't entirely general purpose. They only knew how to play Go. Entrepreneur Guy Suter pointed out that AlphaGo "couldn't just wake up one morning and decide it wants to learn how to use fire-arms."[2] On the other hand, AI researcher Stuart Russell stated, "AI methods are progressing much faster than expected, [which] makes the question of the long-term outcome more urgent....In order to ensure that increasingly powerful AI systems remain completely under human control...there is a lot of work to do."[3]

Stephen Hawking, among others, warned that in the future, self-improving AI could gain actual general intelligence, leading to AI taking over from humans. Others, such as AI expert Jean-Gabriel Ganascia disagree, saying, "Things like 'common sense'...may never be reproducible....I don't see why we would speak about fears. On the contrary, this raises hopes in many domains such as health and space exploration."[4] Computer scientist Richard Sutton seconds this opinion: "I don't think people should be scared...but I do think people should be paying attention."[5]

2   Tracey Lien & Steven Borowiek, "AlphaGo beats human Go champ in milestone for artificial intelligence," Los Angeles *Times*, March 12, 2016, http://www.latimes.com/world/asia/la-fg-korea-alphago-20160312-story.html.

3   Breitbart Tech, "Rise of the Machines: Keep an Eye on AI, Say Experts," March 12, 2016, https://www.breitbart.com/tech/2016/03/12/rise-of-the-machines-keep-an-eye-on-ai-say-experts/.

4   Park Moo-jong, "We are the champions," *Korea Times,* March 1y, 2016, http://www.koreatimes.co.kr/www/common/printpreview.asp?categoryCode=636&newsIdx=200581

5   Tanya Lewis, "An AI expert says Google's Go-playing program is missing 1 key feature of human intelligence," *Business Insider UK,* March 11, 2016, http://uk.businessinsider.com/what-does-googles-deepmind-victory-mean-for-ai-2016-3?r=US&IR=T.

Preprogrammed or specific learning algorithms use manually labeled or curated data to solve specific problems, such as chess moves. By contrast, generalized learning algorithms are able to start programming themselves at a certain point, using unlabeled, uncurated data to create generalized models that can solve a variety of different problems.

Most experts thought AlphaGo's generalized learning model would work by 2020. Then AlphaGo's 2016 release beat world Go champion Lee Sedol five games out of five, four years ahead of schedule. Sedol, who had expected to win at least three of those rounds, said, "I have been playing this game for many, many years, but this is the first time that I actually learned new techniques from the machine."

The success of an algorithm that didn't have any pre-set rules was an a-ha experience for both Sedol and leaders in the industry. AlphaGo had unlocked the potential and hidden patterns within Go data to find new ways to play the game. Every Go player in the world benefited because they learned new ways and got new perspectives on how to play more efficiently.

The Fourth Industrial Revolution seems to have come four years earlier than expected. The applications are unlimited, and it has now become vital to leverage data with machine-intelligence-modeling techniques to sustain and grow your competitive advantage in the market. You and your business can obtain opportunities and insights never previously imagined, meaning you can better plan and enhance your business operations and better serve your customers.

MACHINE INTELLIGENCE: A "BRAIN HELPER"

I would like you to think of machine intelligence as a "brain helper," a tool that can extend and augment our human intelligence. At a Microsoft Ignite event in September 2016, Microsoft CEO Satya Nadella said, "We are pursuing AI so that we can empower every person and every institution that people build with tools of AI so that they can go on to solve the most pressing problems of our society and our economy."

That's the purpose, goal, and real promise of machine intelligence technology.

To solve the most crucial problems of our era, we are going to have to rely on machine intelligence techniques to sort through and process our vast and rapidly increasing store of data. To illustrate the challenge, the average American encounters and attempts to process around ten million data points a day, the equivalent of reading more than 350 newspapers.[6] We don't have time to read all these newspapers. Even if we had the time, would we be able to process all the information and come up with clear, efficient conclusions about what we have read? That's impossible. Even if you had the time, your eyes, brain, and memory could not process all this information properly, in an egalitarian way.

The problem lies in our physical and physiological limitations. Our short-term memory can capture roughly seven data points at a time. If I show you 100 data points, you will likely only catch seven to ten of them, and the data you do catch will be extremely biased because the eye catches specific data with certain colors, sizes, and messages that resonate with our previous experience and attract our attention.

We therefore need to try different techniques for sorting all this information. The solution is using machine intelligence to process this vast amount of data in an egalitarian way since our brains aren't capable of doing so.

We need a tool that will help us, but don't think of this tool as a "robot." Think of it as a servant or another brain that helps you crunch and process ten million data points a day and reduce this huge data set to a much smaller

---

6   Daniel J. Levitin, *The Organized Mind: Thinking Straight in the Age of Information Overload*, Boston: Dutton, 2014.

subset of options, say, seven options that have already been optimized.

Your machine-intelligence brain helper can crunch all the data without prejudice to find the gemstones and gold nuggets hidden within, providing you with an optimized subset of data, and enabling you to evaluate different opportunities efficiently and effectively. Now you have seven options, not ten million, to choose from, and you can then make your choice based on your previous experience, knowledge, intuition, or whatever makes the most sense to you.

You make the final decision, not the machine. Your brain helper will only make recommendations, not replace you, take your job, or make decisions for you. By crunching data and picking out its most crucial elements, the technology provides your business, and humanity, with a human service. That's why I call this the human + machine era.

AI FEAR AND TREMBLING: THE HORROR FILM EFFECT

There's one thing I can't emphasize enough: AI technology is not here to replace human judgment or steal your job. The technology's purpose is not to replace or eliminate the human decision-maker who comes to the problem with vast amount of knowledge, background, experience, and intuition. It's simply a tool that can and will enable you to survive in this era of an overwhelming wealth of data.

As an educator in the field, it's my duty and responsibility to address our love-hate relationship with AI. On the "love-story" side, many people are excited about this new digital world, its benefits and opportunities. At the same time, when discussing AI and machine intelligence, our minds often focus on horror movies and an uneducated perception of the technology's uses and purpose.

2001: A Space Odyssey came out in1986, *Bladerunner* in 1982, and *Ex Machina* in 2009. All these films hinge on the so-called singularity theory, portraying a world in which machines reinvent themselves, become smarter than humans, and then replace us. The fact, from both a research and computational-power perspective, is that we are very far away from that point.

The singularity theory was set forth first in Ray Kurzweil's book *The Singularity Is Near: When Humans Transcend Biology*. People are terrified of the singularity because it supposedly means that machines will soon be controlling the world. People hate AI because Hollywood science-fiction and horror movies often revolve around machines outsmarting and replacing humans. A British Science

Association survey found that one in three respondents believe "that the rise of artificial intelligence is a threat to humanity."[7]

That's a huge misconception. Your business is in danger if you're afraid of machine intelligence because you're not making data-driven decisions. Look at the business decisions you do make: they are almost certainly far from being efficient, optimal, or leading-edge. Why? Because we live in an era where there is an ever-increasing wealth of data, but we can't *process* all of it.

Because you cannot digest and process all this data, you make inefficient—even doomed—decisions every day in your personal and professional lives. If you don't use machine intelligence to help make better, smarter, data-driven decisions, your organization won't survive, and the future of our economy, society, and planet are at risk.

AI has good sides and bad. Take the new, exponentially growing applications of quantum computing, which is not a binary (0 or 1) system but encompasses the infinite spectrum of all the numbers between zero and one. Quantum computing can solve problems, such as in healthcare, that binary supercomputers can't because

---

7   British Science Association, "One in three believe that the rise of artificial intelligence is a threat to humanity," https://www.britishscienceassociation.org/news/rise-of-artificial-intelligence-is-a-threat-to-humanity.

the time needed to find a binary solution to many non-binary real-world problems is almost infinite. Quantum computing can now give us answers to real-life problems we couldn't solve before.

But quantum computing also has a dark side. It can decrypt any encrypted system, which introduces risks and liabilities to secured systems, such as banking and government. What's important here are the designers and creators of this technology and the principles they follow. When companies like IBM and NVIDIA design quantum smart chips and computers, they follow guidelines on how they plan to solve specific problems, say in healthcare, and limit the device's scope to the specific use case. These guidelines are announced publicly, sending the message that these enterprises take full responsibility for these technologies and their effects.

In addressing AI, it's impossible to ignore the common fear that machines will take our jobs, replacing us. Research indicates that automation and smart-learning systems will likely eliminate around 10 percent of today's jobs and that 100 percent of job responsibilities will look different as we progress in the Fourth Industrial Revolution.[8] Job creation is also a critical part of the equation.

8   Sarah Kessler, "An Optimist's Guide to the Robot Revolution," *Quartz*, March 9, 2017, https://qz.com/904285/the-optimists-guide-to-the-robot-apocalypse.

New skills and new jobs will emerge, and unemployment isn't expected to rise.

I am confident that humanity will adapt to the Fourth as to all the previous Industrial Revolutions. The economy will provide enough opportunities for everyone to participate. We just need to make sure these skills are inclusive and not held by one elite group.

THE BENEFITS OF MACHINE INTELLIGENCE

Let's look at early data-science adopters: companies like Google, Facebook, Amazon, and Pandora, with its genome project fifteen years ago. Most were tech companies, but there were one or two long-standing incumbent corporations that were also early adopters.

Looking closely, you can see that these companies have long benefitted from using state-of-the-art machine intelligence to leverage data and gain insights into their businesses and customers. They have learned how to better engage with and serve those customers, how to create new products for them, and how to tailor messages for them. As a result, these early adopters have become leaders in their industries, radically increased their ROI, and now control large markets.

Machine intelligence, fully applied, will exponentially

increase the benefits your business derives from its data. When you dig through all your data, create successful machine-intelligence-modeling techniques, and operationalize them throughout your organization, you will have profoundly leveraged your data assets. Transformation will occur everywhere in the enterprise, and many, if not all departments, will be able to utilize the customer insights you have obtained.

HOW MACHINE INTELLIGENCE IS CURRENTLY BEING LEVERAGED

Today, the most innovative companies rely on data-science and machine-intelligence techniques to drive and add value to business processes and user experience. When I ask executives what type of company Amazon is, they usually say, "Amazon is everything." This is somewhat true, but if you really dig in, you'll see that Amazon is essentially an enormous supply-chain company. They then took their long supply chain and created modeling techniques to optimize data in every link of this chain.

Eventually, this huge, interconnected chain became extremely efficient and better able to serve Amazon's customers and users. Amazon perfected machine intelligence in every part of its large supply-chain structure.

Consider, for instance, how Amazon optimizes one part

of its supply chain, its warehouses. In a medium-size Amazon warehouse or distribution center, millions of packages go in and out every day. Can you imagine one person or even an army of 500 people trying to figure out how to organize millions of packages going in and out of a warehouse efficiently? It's impossible. By leveraging data with modeling techniques, Amazon warehouses can optimally store and enable those million packages to route in and out to their proper destinations.[9]

Alibaba, the Chinese Amazon, does the same thing: employing robots to quickly organize their large warehouse facilities.[10] Learning algorithms tell the robots how to organize millions of packages efficiently so that when a truck comes, they can load it quickly and start shipping seamlessly.

Another area, among many others, where Amazon uses modeling techniques is delivery time. Amazon leverages parsed data to tell us exactly when we can expect to see our packages on our doorsteps. They have a long history of shipping items across the world, which provides

---

9   Will Knight, "Inside Amazon's Warehouse, Human-Robot Symbiosis," *MIT Technology Review,* July 7, 2015, https://www.technologyreview.com/s/538601/inside-amazons-warehouse-human-robot-symbiosis/; James Vincent, "Welcome to the Automated Warehouse of the Future," *The Verge,* May 8, 2018, https://www.theverge.com/2018/5/8/17331250/automated-warehouses-jobs-ocado-andover-amazon.

10   James Pickering, "Take a Look Inside Alibaba's Smart Warehouse Where Robots Do 70% of the Work," *Business Insider,* September 19, 2017, https://www.businessinsider.com/inside-alibaba-smart-warehouse-robots-70-per-cent-work-technology-logistics-2017-9.

an enormous amount of data. They also have access to weather data and can predict when their vehicles need maintenance. All this data taken together allows them to predict, with great accuracy, when a package will be at our door.

Netflix has excelled for years at leveraging data to provide movie recommendations. Every time you go to Netflix, you see your movie recommendations on the first screen, and the company has done a great job of making selections you will resonate with. Facebook has also perfected this, finding the right content and advertisements for the right users, based on their preferences, by applying machine intelligence techniques to the curated data in its news feeds. Google searches do much the same thing. Every time we Google something, we get highly resonant results.

MACHINE INTELLIGENCE: THE FUTURE OF BUSINESS INNOVATION

Although machine intelligence is already being used today, the potential it holds for business innovation in the future is even more interesting. The future of business innovation has machine intelligence at its core, driving product development and user experience.

A prime example is Nest, the latest generation of thermostat. Products like this are designed from the inside out, not the outside in. Nest is a machine-intelligence device that connects to your phone. It knows when you are close to home because the phone automatically connects to your router, while simultaneously receiving external data, such as the weather. You play with Nest for two weeks, giving it feedback on whether the room temperature is too warm or cold. The machine-intelligence device learns from this input and other data it collects, and after two weeks, you have a device that serves you without your needing to touch it. Nest must be doing something right since it is already selling millions of units. It's a product built entirely around machine intelligence at its core.

Other examples are Spotify and Amazon Echo. Both rely heavily on machine intelligence techniques to create, sell, and make recommendations that serve users better, which is why they're so popular.

CHAPTER 2

———

DEMYSTIFYING MACHINE INTELLIGENCE

Consider a process every executive and business leader is familiar with: the OODA loop—Observe, Orient, Decide, and Act. The OODA loop is critical concept to rapid and agile learning.[11] Military strategist John Boyd helped create the concept and argued, both mathematically and intuitively, that the faster you iterate on the OODA loop, the faster you will win or achieve your goal, even though you will make mistakes along the way.

John Boyd was a jet fighter pilot. He wanted to create an intuitive system that could be used in a war scenario where two fighter jets try to intercept one another. He

---

11   Wikipedia, s.v. "OODA loop," https://en.wikipedia.org/wiki/OODAloop. August 2, 2018,

believed that the most interesting and agile learning process in this situation would be to observe the scene, orient our minds, decide on an action, then act to see if the action has the desired outcome or not, and run this loop again and again.

Boyd argued that, as long as you iterate this loop, and despite any mistakes made along the way, you will eventually win. You can shoot a missile that doesn't hit the target or embark on a project that can't be implemented, but as long as you learn from your mistakes and your mind remains agile, you will eventually win by iterating the loop. This a great analogy for machine intelligence, since all machine-intelligence models operate like OODA loops.

Machine-intelligence models observe the data we have and orient around an initial point. That is, they choose a random starting point in a given data space and then make moves based on their mathematical relations to the data, beginning at and moving beyond the chosen starting point. This process yields information that can be acted upon.

Think of a robot that tries to flip pancakes. Before it begins to act, it has been fed data on how to flip pancakes. The pancake-flipping robot hand has a certain range of movement, can apply more force or less, and so on.

The first thousand tries, the robot can't flip the pancake. It's either too fast or too forceful, and the half-cooked pancake falls out of the pan. The robot makes a lot of mistakes along the way but eventually learns from experience, iterating the OODA loop. Eventually, it perfects all the parameters of efficient flipping. The robot now flips pancakes perfectly, without burning or dropping them on the floor.

It takes our brains time to learn. Think about how long it took you to learn to use a knife and fork. We eventually accomplish the task because we learn how to think about and solve problems from experience over time.

It's the same with machine learning. Although machine learning tends to be extraordinarily agile, it still takes time. In the Orient phase, the machine, at first, chooses a random point in the data space, but eventually, over time, this random point will converge to what data scientists call a global minima, the most efficient and optimal point in space.[12] When you reach a global minima, you have found the best way to solve a problem.

The machine will make mistakes while learning, like humans do, but, also like humans, most of the time the machine will ultimately be able to perfect the task.

---

12   That is, in those instances when a global minima can be found mathematically.

With machine learning, the process can often happen extremely quickly, although this is not always the case.

HOW GOOGLE PERFECTED THE OODA LOOP FOR ROI

Google is a company that perfected the OODA loop to increase ROI. An example is a search I did a year and a half ago on "machine learning," which yielded two different top results: The first was an advertisement for an Intel product called "machine learning." Second was another machine-learning advertisement for a company called Apttus.

Machine Learning - Intel® Data Analytics - intel.com
[Ad] www.intel.com/**MachineLearning** ▾
Learn About Machine Learning with Intel. Find Tools, Videos, Briefs & More.
Ready-to-Use Algorithms · Intel® Architecture · Intel® Developer Zone
    Machine Learning Video   Intel® MKL
    Intel IT Peer Network   Intel® Developer Zone

Guide to Machine Learning - Official Apttus™ Site - apttus.com
[Ad] info.apttus.com/ ▾
Learn How to Use **Machine Learning** to Grow Your Enterprise Company. Free Guide!
Smarter Analytics · Drive Business Outcomes · Strategic Growth

Why did my search come up with Intel and Apttus? Why was Intel first and Apttus second? Why not NVIDIA or some other machine-learning advertisement? When I ask executives these questions, 95 percent say that Intel came up first in my search because they paid Google the most—more than Apttus—so Google ranked it higher.

That's the common answer. However, Google actually

displayed the two advertisements based on an optimization method that gave results based on the likelihood of me clicking on them, which was in turn based on my user preferences. If you tried to approach this problem in a conventional business fashion, the formula would be different. It would revolve around user preferences displayed *after* clicking on the advertisement, maximizing Google's revenue.

This simple, even superficial, example demonstrates sophisticated modeling techniques. To a certain extent, Google employs the "multi-armed bandit" algorithm used in every casino in the world, which is based on the concept of exploitation versus exploration.

Casinos exploit you, explore opportunities with you, and take your money. When you enter a casino, you hear a constant loud refrain of "bling, bling, bling." People are shouting happily, and you know they're winning. The casino exploits opportunities with you as you enter by placing machines there that give you a high probability of winning a small amount of money. After you feel "lucky" or that you have a "hot hand," you are tempted to explore the rest of the casino, where large halls containing higher-stakes games require you to bet more if you want to play. The catch is that your probability of winning these high-stakes games is lower. You first are being exploited—easy wins that are small for the casino—and then start to explore—large wins for the casino—which demonstrates the "multi-armed bandit" concept.

So why did Google show me advertisements for Intel and Apttus? Yes, both companies pay Google substantial amounts of money, but there's more to it than that. Google both exploits us and gets us to explore opportunities to maximize their revenue. How?

Google knows I'm familiar with Intel because of my search history, and therefore, I'm more likely to click on an Intel ad. With each click, they make money. This is an easy way to exploit an opportunity and generate revenue. They, then showed a second advertisement for a company I was less familiar with called Apttus, which was outside my search history.

Apttus is an opportunity for Google to get me to explore. I'm not exploring a random subject because machine learning already resonates with me. Based on my preferences, they're attempting to get me to explore something that I don't yet know about and therefore might be tempted to click on and generate extra revenue for Google.

Essentially, Google is double-dipping. They dip with Intel because of the high likelihood that I'll click, given my history and familiarity with the company, and they double-dip because there's a high chance I'll click on Apttus as well out of curiosity. This intuitive exploitation-and-exploration learning algorithm that iterates on user data every few milliseconds enables Google to maximize revenue. It's how Google became one of the largest companies in the world.

MACHINE INTELLIGENCE'S CURRENT SHORTCOMINGS

Machine intelligence models provide many exciting opportunities, but there are shortcomings in today's techniques as well. This is not to discourage you in any way but is something you should be aware of.

LABELED DATA

Most current machine-intelligence models are trained to work most efficiently and quickly with labeled, structured data. This requires the data to be observed and labeled prior to input. For instance, the data identifying spam email must be precisely labeled, and the machine needs a lot of this data to identify spam properly. If you have massive data sets, it can take months to label it all properly.

To run machine-intelligence models on a doctor's prescriptions, for example, we need to input prescriptions and other documents done in her handwriting that have already been decoded. Someone has to have decoded the handwriting, which is to say that a human has to label the data before it can be input, and we need a lot of such labeled data to run the machine-learning model. (More detail on this process can be found in Appendix B.)

Most machine-learning techniques need to be initially trained with labeled data, and most data sets are not labeled, which creates a problem. "Deep-learning" neural networks, an advanced form of machine intelligence discussed in greater depth in Chapter 8 and Appendix B, need to be trained with labeled data first before they can start training themselves, that is, before they can start analyzing and learning from unlabeled data.

So companies need to invest in a substantial amount of time in labeling data. You also need to have a diverse and comprehensive data set to make machine-intelligence predictions efficient and accurate.

TRANSPARENCY

The other drawback of these techniques is their relative incomprehensibility. People call machine learning a black box because it's hard to explain in simple language how the machine arrives at certain decisions or outcomes. This is different, for instance, from statistics, which is also a complicated subject, but one that allows us to trace how condition x led or will lead to outcome y. We often can't do this in studying machine intelligence.

The input and output layers of a deep-learning neural network can be observed, but this isn't necessarily true of the many layers in between, in which data flows in a non-linear fashion. Of course, we could say the same thing about our own brains: despite many advances in neuroscience, we still don't really know how they work.

This black-box aspect of machine learning is one reason so few self-driving cars are allowed on the streets. If an accident were to occur, we wouldn't know—from a modeling or mathematical perspective—what led to the accident. We'd know there was an accident, but we couldn't trace exactly how the data moving in between the input and output layers caused the accident to occur.

Creating more transparency around the relationship between a "black box's" input and output is quite possible. However, with complex models, such transparency requires a lot of expensive computational power.

There is a trade-off here. If you want the system to be more transparent, it will cost more time and money. On the other hand, a black box will give you results faster and more cheaply, potentially discovering ever-more unique patterns due to high usage of computational power to analyze the data. This trade-off will be overcome in time through more research and increases in computational power, but it remains a real issue today.

LEARNING REUSABILITY

An even more significant limitation of today's machine intelligence is "learning reusability." From an early age, we humans discover that we can apply certain lessons learned in a specific context to a wide variety of different contexts. But machine-intelligence models trained on one data set can't necessarily carry their experiences and learning to another.

Take, for example, the recommendation engine Facebook created for its content. Could we take Facebook's content-recommendation engine and use it as the basis of creating another recommendation engine in a completely different field, such as recommending content to Tesla drivers or soldiers involved in military operations?

More broadly, could we apply the learning in one vertical of the business—based on a specific, curated data set—to other verticals with different data sets within the same enterprise? Probably not, because the machine was trained and optimized on the first specific set of curated data. Once the data set drastically changes, the machine will start making mistakes again because this is a new, unfamiliar input. Machine-intelligence models are specific rather than general. If we attempt to create too general a model, its predictions will not be accurate enough to satisfy the initial problem or goal.

On the other hand—as you will see later—if a model is too specific, new data may break it. There's a trade-off between generalization and specificity. Since we must make each model just specific enough, there's a problem transferring learning from one model to another. So organizations must repeatedly commit resources to train new models with new data, even if the use cases or problems involved seem similar.

THE BUSINESS LEADER'S ROLE IN THE FOURTH INDUSTRIAL REVOLUTION

One of business leaders' primary roles in the twenty-first century is to champion data. You need to set your employees an example of a data-first approach. Every time they make a suggestion or recommendation that can lead or contribute to a decision or outcome, you must ask them for the data supporting their recommendations. Hold them accountable.

Always get people to show you the data before you make a decision or come to a conclusion. This data-first approach will drive more data-driven decision-making throughout the organization. I always tell executives, "Listen, you are a group of twenty-five people managing 65,000 people or more. Start to ask the people you manage for data." This creates a positive feedback loop that amplifies the approach. Your team will go from asking for data once a day to looking at data a hundred times a day. If a top executive asks her direct reports for data, her voice will be amplified throughout the organization as they ask their direct reports for data as well.

This is how you start embedding the data-driven mindset into your corporate culture. Make sure your employees have reviewed the data and can adequately explain their decisions, recommendations, and options before they come to you.

Another important role for twenty-first-century business leaders is applying machine-intelligence techniques and a data-driven mindset horizontally. If you have solved a problem such as predictive maintenance for warehouse equipment, you should ask yourself whether you can apply the same solutions to consumer products. Maybe the data involved is not that different. Within the same organization, user behavior patterns will be similar enough that previous learning can be applied.

Diffusing machine intelligence horizontally through different parts of the organization can leverage its predictive power. Reusing learning in completely different verticals outside the organization is unlikely. But if Amazon builds a predictive maintenance model for its warehouses, perhaps they can extend predictive maintenance to the vehicles that interact with the warehouses and so on throughout the ecosystem.

You also need to constantly refine your data strategy. You must focus not only on the technology required to pull data from different systems within the organization but on data availability and acquisition. You can't just create a strategy for leveraging data. To add ROI, you also have to think about data availability, accessibility, acquisition, and labeling. Data governance also plays a major strategic role.

Because data science changes so quickly, business leaders must keep learning. Machine intelligence is a fast-growing field, evolving right now, even as you are reading. You should familiarize yourself with the capabilities of today's tools and where short-term advantages are likely to occur. But also get a sense of where the field is heading and develop a perspective on what the longer-term future might look like for your organization. Be curious, adopt an agile mindset, and stay tuned in to trends in this rapidly evolving industry.

CHAPTER 3

DATA-DRIVEN ORGANIZATIONS

To thrive in the Fourth Industrial Revolution, business leaders must first understand machine intelligence and then focus on creating a data-driven culture. You need to act in three different dimensions to transform your organization into a data- and model-driven enterprise. The first dimension is the *data* itself, the second is *technology* infrastructure, and the third is *people, process, and culture.*

First, create and communicate transparent organizational goals that both your technical and non-technical staffs can understand. Companies will succeed in the machine-intelligence era only when their leadership teams have **clear goals, define what success looks like**, and **ask the right questions.** Defining what success looks like will help your technical people choose the proper targets and correct modeling techniques. Asking the right questions will give them a context so that they can be sure that when they pick a model, they choose one that is aligned with your business goals and adds direct value to the organization.

Second, as has been said before, set an example for your employees by championing data. People look up to you. When you champion a data-first approach, it will be amplified throughout the entire organization.

Third, build a healthy culture and environment in which your technical team can flourish and thrive. Many organizations don't know what this looks like because they don't understand that their technical team fills a vital research role. When I talk to startups, I always tell them, "Never hire only a single data scientist because he or she won't survive." This is because, working in a research-oriented field, we data scientists need to collaborate. Create channels to enhance collaboration between cross-functional teams of data scientists and get into the habit of making data-driven decisions by bringing data and decisions closer together.

WHAT IS A DATA- AND MODEL-DRIVEN ORGANIZATION?

A data- and model-driven organization is an enterprise that cultivates a culture of continuously using data and machine-intelligence techniques to make *all* business decisions. Data-driven refers to the first steps in the intelligence maturity curve, where data is leveraged descriptively to generate reports and to do monitoring and periodic analysis. Model-driven refers to orchestrating predictive and prescriptive-analytic capabilities for automating interactions in real time. These stages are illustrated in the following figure.

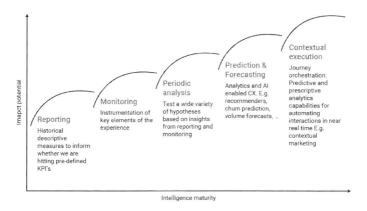

A data- and model-driven organization is an enterprise that cultivates a culture of continuously using data and machine-intelligence techniques to make *all* business decisions. "Data-driven" refers to leveraging all *current* data in the service of your business. "Model-driven" takes this a step further: machine-intelligence algorithms and techniques process the data to make predictions of *future* trends.

When I ask executives what a data-driven organization is,

99 percent typically say it's an organization that makes decisions with data. They forget the main point, which is that a data-driven organization makes *all* business decisions with data.

These are the decisions that add real value to your business and align with your organization's top goals. First, define your goals in a data-driven manner, and then make business decisions by leveraging data and modeling techniques.

Executives and business leaders know what their business problems are. In workshops, when I ask them to write down their top four business problems, they're always able to do so. In working with many large enterprises, I have also discovered that data can solve each one of these problems.

When asked in workshops, executives intuitively say, "I've got four major business problems. Three of them can be solved with data. The fourth problem is different." I then show them exactly how the remaining problem can be solved with data. They just haven't fully learned how to turn business problems into data problems.

Executives believe 75 percent of their business problems, a substantial number, can be solved with data, but not the other 25 percent. There's a knowledge gap here. Eventually, if we bridge this gap, data will be able to solve 100 percent of business problems. It boils down to better educating executives on how to adopt a machine-intelligence mindset. The more we push organizations toward data-driven models, the better.

Transforming an organization involves a big cultural and management change. Culture and processes are critical. When transforming culture, you need to start with yourself. When faced with business decisions, many executives try to predict the next, best step. They ask, "Okay, what do I think will happen in the future?"

This approach is wrong because it is not data-driven. Executives must begin changing their corporate cultures by changing themselves, moving from the mindset of, "This is what I think is going to happen in the future," to the mindset of, "This is what I know." "What I know" always means returning to the data, to past trends. Determine current trends and orient yourself to possible outcomes with data. Then you can make effective business decisions. Once you enact this cultural change within yourself, you can start changing the entire organization.

THE CHALLENGES TO BUILDING A DATA-DRIVEN ORGANIZATION

The problem is *you*, or rather *us*.

What are the barriers to transforming your organization into a data-driven enterprise? Executives don't always understand the transformation has to start with themselves. If you want to understand this space, funding will be required. If you don't understand how to translate your business problems into data problems, your organization won't be able to transform.

This is a people, process, and culture problem, and business leaders are directly in charge of all these issues. So one of the main barriers to solving these problems lies within the operations and business side of the enterprise rather than the data or technology side. This is not a data problem or a technical problem, as many executives would like to think.

A data- and model-driven enterprise can respond quickly to all the predictions and information that come from sophisticated machine-intelligence models. If your organization is not agile enough to respond quickly to these models' predictions, you won't get any added value from your investment in machine-intelligence applications.

Another question I ask in workshops is why it's so hard to become a data-driven organization. The answer, again, is that there is a management issue. We are all ignorant in certain areas. Executives are not accustomed to solving problems with data. You're accustomed to solving problems by tapping into your experience, gut feelings, and heuristics. You're not used to saying, "Show me the data. Show me the predictions. Show me the trends. Then I'll make my decision."

Control is another reason it's hard for organizations to become data-driven. Executives want maximum control, especially when it comes to decision-making. Sometimes the data will show you a completely different path to follow, which can make things difficult. Executives often have a "my way or the highway" attitude, but sometimes, the data will conflict with your intuition and experience, and this lack of control can annoy and even trigger executives.

Another negative factor is impatience. Executives want results now, but that's not how machine learning works. Since machine intelligence intrepidly attempts to mimic our brains, it needs time to learn and produce the correct output, making mistakes and learning from them along the way. This iterative OODA-loop process takes time.

Yet another problem is fear. Most executives are not technical, do not come from engineering or data-related backgrounds, and often fear data. They suffer from information overload, especially executives whose background is law or another field that traditionally doesn't require a lot of work with numbers. This is a massive issue. People must overcome their fear of data and get into the habit of making decisions by looking at numbers.

The last issue is attention. The current wealth of data creates an attention-span problem because we're confronted by so many options. We try to digest a surplus of information every day so it's difficult to focus and orient our minds, understand what the data tells us, and isolate ourselves from surrounding noise in order to make healthy, data-driven decisions.

To mitigate these issues, executives must develop a data-science or machine-intelligence mindset. To start the machine-intelligence and data-science journey, first identify all your business problems and figure out which ones you can feasibly translate into data and modeling problems. Then your technical team can act to help solve them. Once you start getting your team into the habit, they will solve more and more business problems by leveraging data and modeling techniques, and your organization will gradually become data driven.

Executives also need to understand data-science workflow. You do not have to train yourself to become a data scientist, but you do need to develop a critical mindset. You must understand what happens in each phase of the machine-intelligence process so you can, first, give the right instructions and, then, analyze and critique the output or results.

WHAT EXECUTIVES MUST DO IN THE MACHINE-INTELLIGENCE ERA

From my experience working closely with both technical and non-technical leaders, I've observed that those who succeed in leveraging current technology: (1) set clear goals, (2) define what success looks like, and (3) ask the right questions before embarking on a machine-intelligence initiative. Such clear direction enables technical teams to understand and translate business objectives and problems into solvable data and modeling problems.

I always say to business leaders that, as a data scientist, if my manager provides me these three inputs, my life will be much easier. Now, I can easily translate the business problem into hard-core modeling techniques and math and make a real impact on the organization.

To see how a business problem is translated into simple math, look at the formula below:

$$\text{Prob}\left(\underset{i}{y_i} = 1 | X\right) =$$

(1)

↓

Set the right goal

(3) Ask the right Q's.

One: Set a clear goal. In the formula above, y_i represents the goal of the analysis or business problem. Say that Apple would like to forecast the demand for a new product line. An Apple executive wants to figure out whether customers will buy an iPhoneXS or an iPhoneX, both products on which Apple has and owns the data. In this case, the executive would like to find out the probability or likelihood that a customer will by the iPhoneXS, given all information and data Apple has about its customers and products.

To head in the right direction, I, as a data scientist, need to construct a mathematical model that involves a simple binary choice: either 0 or 1. If the customer buys an iPhoneXS, the result is 1. This is the mathematical expression of the outcome, which captures the core business goal of the analysis.

Two: Define what success looks like. I can now set a target for the analysis, which is that y_i (the goal or output) is equal to 1 (the customer bought an iPhoneXS). The X in the equation $y_i = 1 \mid X$ captures all the data and information we have that might explain a customer buying an iPhoneXS rather than an iPhoneX. These could include features such as battery life, product design features, brand aspects, purchase history, and so on. All this data is input into the model.

In short, once I understand both the business problem and set the target or desired outcome, the problem can be translated into mathematics and the correct mathematical model formulated. In mathematical terms, we can now define what success looks like for the analysis: it is when we set y_i equal to 1, that is, the iPhoneXS. We want to understand what contributes to the likelihood of the consumer buying an iPhoneXS as opposed to an iPhoneX.

Three: Asking the right questions. The formulation and construction of the mathematical model, derived from a purely business-oriented question and problem, can now be matched with the machine-intelligence models that will help us solve the problem. In this case, a logistic regression model was chosen to help determine the probability, based on all available data, that a customer will buy an iPhoneXS.

EMBRACING DATA-DRIVEN DECISIONS

When I conduct workshops behind closed doors to help executives embrace data-driven decisions, I typically ask, "How would you embrace data-driven decision-making?" Most of the time, they respond, "Look at the data." Fantastic answer! But where is the data? How available is the data when it's time for you to make a decision and act?

One great way to make sure such data is available is actually very simple: create your own data dashboard. The dashboard will provide a snapshot of the data in your enterprise in relation to the metrics or goals you want to monitor. This could be revenue, number of leads, conversion rates, closed deals, cash flow, and so on.

The dashboard will help you get a sense—a snapshot—of where your organization stands by looking at various data inputs. When a decision has to be made, you will quickly be able to orient your mind and make informed business decisions.

Most enterprises work with third-party data-utilization platform and tools, such as Salesforce, Tableau, Oracle, or SAP. Most of these have embedded customized-dashboard capabilities. Such dashboards can be created with a few clicks. As these tools are business-oriented, creating your own personalized, customized dashboard will not be rocket science.

I both urge and challenge you to create your own dashboard. Most times, technical teams create metrics-visualization dashboards for executives. The problem is that because the executives didn't build the dashboards themselves, they find them hard to use or interpret. You don't need to know how to code to create a simple dashboard on your own. You don't need to know anything other than how to choose the right metrics and drag data across a screen. It's simple and impactful. Make sure you have easy access to the dashboard so the data you need to make a data-driven decision is only a click away.

STOP MAKING EXCUSES AND OVERCOME INERTIA

Most executives, when asked what the problem in becoming a data-driven organization is and why they don't start this change immediately, often blame the data and technology infrastructure rather than themselves. As a business leader, you need to recognize and acknowledge such behavior. Realize that this is a learning problem for which you yourself are responsible.

Large incumbent organizations really don't have data or technology-infrastructure problems. Look at Fortune 500 companies. On average, most of them have been operating for more than eighty years. They've accumulated a lot of data during that time, especially in recent years, when everything has been digitally tracked.

In my experience working with many of the world's top corporations, I've found that executives can be contrary. They say they don't like the data and start shopping around. They claim the data they have isn't good enough.

Stop searching for data and, at least for a while, focus on the tremendous amount of data you already have. To take two examples, from your inventory records, you already know how many units of a certain product you've sold, when you sold them, and to whom. There is also a tremendous amount of data about problems with your products in your web-based help desk. If you start leveraging this data, you'll see you already have quite a lot, and this will help you push your organization forward from a data-modeling perspective.

Most incumbent organizations generate revenue of many millions or even billions of dollars. They have established partnerships with major technology companies like IBM, Intel, or Dell. They have a lot of resources and have no problem calling these companies and implementing state-of-the-art technology in their organizations. They have the technology as well as the data. So why can't these organizations quickly transform themselves to become data- and model-driven? Because of people and culture, these are operation and process problems.

Overcome your inertia. Get into the habit of making data-driven decisions by asking, "What do I know?" rather than "What do I think?" Change your mindset and habits, always refer to the data, look at your dashboard before you make business decisions, and champion data every time you are about to make one. When your direct reports tell you, "You should do x, y, and z," you should ask them what the data says before you make the decision.

Embody this mindset and these habits yourself so that when people come to you, they'll understand how you think. The next time they come to present something to you, they'll think harder about figuring out what they need to show you to help you make the right decision.

There's an exercise I typically do with executives during my workshops. "You're here to think," I'd say, and then ask, "How can you, as a leader, better embrace data-driven decision-making?"

Many very smart executives often respond by saying they're clueless. Then I talk about the dashboard, a great way to get a snapshot of the data in their organizations in order to make data-driven decisions.

In these workshops, I then ask how obstacles in making more data-driven decisions can be overcome. Each organization has different issues, which means each executive's answer will be different as well. Remember, it's not about the data or technology: it's about you and your people. You need to get into the habit of asking where the data is, but how this is done will be different in every organization. As a leader, you need to inspire your people to change their culture.

The evidence is clear: data-driven decisions are better decisions. Business leaders will either embrace this fact or be replaced by others who do. In the Fourth Industrial Revolution, in sector after sector, companies that figure out how to combine human expertise with data science and machine-intelligence techniques will ultimately win.

CHAPTER 4

DATA-DRIVEN
TRANSFORMATION:
SIX PRINCIPLES

Harnessing information so your organization can become a data- and model-driven enterprise is not a simple task. Many organizations are troubled and don't know where to start and how to embark on the journey successfully. There are six basic principles that will help you figure out where to begin and how to begin expanding your thoughts about transforming your organization, because becoming a data-driven enterprise requires a plan as well as the right culture, people and process, and technology. The goal of transforming your organization to become a data-and-model driven enterprise is to enable it to respond quickly and optimally to the predictions being generated by sophisticated modeling techniques to generate ROI.

These six principles are not a playbook or magic formula for your organization. They are based on and derived from case studies of how other successful companies from various industries have made the transformation successfully.

To summarize the six principles:

1. Data strategy
2. Data democratization, which is one of the biggest gaps organizations are currently experiencing
3. A data- and model-driven culture
4. "Speed to insight": how to derive insights from your data as quickly as possible
5. Data science value as a key performance indicator (KPI)
6. Data governance, security, and privacy

PRINCIPLE ONE: DATA STRATEGY

Start, as always, with your business objectives. Once these are clear, you can design a roadmap and develop a strategy for leveraging the data you already have. It bears repeating that you should always start with what you already have. Data is the gold of the Fourth Industrial Revolution: your competitive advantage. Since your data contains hidden insights, you need to treat it as a strategic asset. So design a roadmap with a clear strategy on how to leverage your data and treat it as a strategic asset across and throughout your organization.

According to Ginni Rometty, CEO and Charmain of IBM, only "20 percent of the data is searchable."[13] The rest, 80 percent, is behind the firewall. This is your proprietary data and your competitive advantage over your competitors. You already sit on a lot of hidden information about your customers, clients, and business that can help you transform your organization and take it to the next level if—and only if—you treat your data as a strategic asset informing all your business decisions.

Typically, when I talk about data strategy with business leaders, their immediate response is, "Hey, this means I'll have to realign the entire organization. How would that work? How can I align all my 100,000 people with a single data strategy?"

However, setting data strategy is different from goal-setting. With goal-setting, we start at the top. Everything must orient to the goals top executives have set for the entire organization for the year. Data strategy, however, can be different for each sub-team and still contribute to the solution of your top business problems. These

---

13   Elizabeth Gurdus, "IBM CEO Ginni Rometty says 80% of the world's data is where the 'real gold' is," June 20, 2017, https://www.cnbc.com/2017/06/20/ibm-ceo-says-80-percent-of-the-worlds-data-is-where-the-real-gold-is.html.

different strategies don't need to involve a single set of constraints.

Of course, everyone must report to and align with top business problems. But when you develop data strategy, do so on a micro level for a specific group or a vertical within the company. Because each vertical has different types of data, you can't establish a single data strategy for the entire organization. Each group within the organization should develop its own data strategy. These should be in line with your business goals, but the multiple data strategies within an organization don't have to be linked into a single, overarching whole.

A prime example of someone who successfully mastered this principle is D. J. Patil, who was the first White House Chief Information Officer under President Obama. Patil treated data as a strategic asset in government and required government data be leveraged to inform policy, improve budgeting, and make operational decisions.[14] He held everyone who reported to him accountable to data and data-driven decision-making. But the data strategies of different government departments were necessarily different from one another.

---

14 D.J. Patil, "A Memo to the American People from U.S. Chief Data Scientist Dr. DJ Patil," February 20, 2015, https://obamawhitehouse.archives.gov/blog/2015/02/19/memo-american-people-us-chief-data-scientist-dr-dj-patil; Anmol Rajpurohit, "White House sees Data as the 21st Century Catalyst for Effective Policing," *KD Nuggets,* May 2015, https://www.kdnuggets.com/2015/05/white-house-police-data-initiative.html.

PRINCIPLE TWO: DATA DEMOCRATIZATION

The second principle is democratizing your data throughout the organization. Data needs to be democratized and made accessible because everyone, from the barista to the CEO, makes business decisions on a daily basis. We know that data-driven decisions are better decisions, so why wouldn't you provide people with access to the data to make better decisions?

However, we live in a world of constraints and regulations. Not all organizations can completely democratize their data, particularly in industries like banking, insurance, and healthcare. Data leakage in these cases would be catastrophic because of privacy issues. It would introduce direct business risk and liability.

The second constraint circles back to the concept that data is gold and a key to your enterprise's competitive advantage. If data is such an important asset, you clearly don't want to share all your data with the entire organization because it might leak out and you would lose that advantage.

So how can we democratize data intelligently? The answer is to figure out how to provide the relevant data to the relevant decision-makers to enhance their decision-making. Look at people's roles, identify what decisions they make on a daily basis, and then provide them with the data that will support these decisions. Providing the right data to the right decision-makers will enhance decision-making.

Don't democratize everything to everyone. Democratize the right data to the right people. Many organizations have done an outstanding job creating a role-based system, whose architecture links roles to decisions and then provides the people who fill those roles with the data needed for making those decisions.

After identifying roles and providing the right people access to the right data, you must also build a technology infrastructure that can handle a high-velocity flood of data and route it efficiently and securely across the organization to individuals and cross-functional teams.

Airbnb did this extraordinarily well, as described in the excellent article "Democratizing Data at Airnbnb."[15] They created a platform on which employees can search for a specific feature or variable and find its details and associated descriptive metadata. You'll also find contact information on the people within the organization who own the data, so you can reach out to them if you want access to it.

---

15   Chris Williams, Eli Brumbaugh, Jeff Feng, John Bodley, and Michelle Thomas, "Democratizing Data at Airbnb," *Medium*, May 12, 2017, https://medium.com/airbnb-engineering/democratizing-data-at-airbnb-852d76c51770.

Airbnb employees can also apply filters to build dashboards that will show what each group in the company is working on from a data perspective. The dashboard gives an overview of the group, the curated content and data they're using, and summary statistics, as illustrated below.

Context and metadata

Employee-centric data view

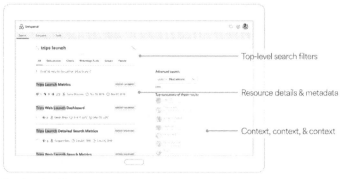

Search-engine data

Team-centric data view

Most organizations today struggle with democratizing data because they don't have metadata in place that properly categorizes and describes the data itself. One of the first things to do in creating a data-driven enterprise is to create a well-defined, precise metadata scheme, setting forth the specific terms and parameters that classify your data.

Your technology team will of course be responsible for setting up the metadata scheme that will help you locate the data you want more easily. However, it's up to senior executives to prioritize and support this. Once the metadata is in place, you can map it onto any goals and decision-making processes you have identified. This will take time and money, but if it isn't implemented, your organization is bound to start losing a lot more of both.

PRINCIPLE THREE: BUILDING A DATA-DRIVEN CULTURE

Principle three is about creating a data-science and analytics culture within the organization. Leaders must incentivize employees to cultivate the habit of looking at data whenever they make decisions, which I call "the point of action." This is tightly linked to the corporate culture you build. I often suggest that executives get creative and set up competitions and rewards for employees who champion data.

A second component of this principle, and one of the biggest current gaps in industry, is bringing technical and non-technical teams closer together, working seamlessly to realize and operationalize machine intelligence to achieve ROI. The gap between technical and non-technical teams remains significant at this point. These teams don't understand each other or know how to work together. This is a major problem that must be faced and overcome.

Nevertheless, there are early adopters, such as Google, that provide great examples of companies that have bridged the gap between its technical and non-technical teams. One of the remedies is educating both teams about each other's roles and functions. The second is a smart, highly collaborative, embedded organizational work structure that requires the two teams to interact during the normal course of business. The third is creating a semi-technical role for a middleman (or middle-woman) between the two sides of the business. This interesting tactic is becoming increasingly popular and proving quite effective.

Some organizations call these people data translators; others call them data-science analysts. You can expect this increasingly essential role to grow and become even more important in the next few years. It bridges the current technical/non-technical gap, helping people translate business problems into data and modeling problems while enabling engineers to orient their minds to technical solutions for business problems they otherwise wouldn't be aware of or understand. We'll return to this important topic in Chapter 10.

PRINCIPLE 4: ACCELERATING SPEED TO INSIGHT

This principle involves unleashing insight as a service quickly and dynamically. The idea is to democratize information and insight about your business through-out the organization. If you provide high-speed, dynamic insight to decision-makers, they will get into the habit of making data-driven decisions. Recall the definition of a data-driven organization: an organization that cultivates a culture of looking at data to make *all* business decisions.

One of the simplest and best ways to unleash insight throughout the organization is to use dynamic dashboard tools that provide insight into and beyond the data. Many organizations do not emphasize the importance and usefulness of such solutions. You already have ability to create dashboards that dynamically represent data and are simple to read and understand. Organizations need to move away from static summaries and reports. They are no longer dynamic enough to inform decision-making.

As you progress along the data-intelligence maturity curve, begin to unleash not only data but machine learning as a service. Democratizing machine learning as a service throughout your organization can be a powerful way to help everyone in your organization—including your non-technical team—to start making more predictive decisions based on machine-learning models.

A dashboard gives you a current perspective of your data in a static or descriptive way. A machine-learning-as-a-service platform will help you move from a descriptive perspective to a dynamic, predictive . Building an environment where everyone can deploy machine-learning models on demand is another major step forward, especially for non-technical teams who don't know how to code but will now be able to get sophisticated machine-intelligence predictions in real time. This puts predictive power and forecasting abilities in everyone's hands, which is one reason why IBM's Watson is so successful.

Uber is an example of a company that did a great job creating a machine-learning-as-a-service platform.[16] This environment enables internal teams to seamlessly build, deploy, and operate machine-learning solutions at the scale Uber requires. It is designed to cover machine-learning workflow from end to end: to manage data; train, evaluate, and deploy models; and make and monitor predictions.

Uber employees can now leverage external data and deploy machine-learning models within the platform ecosystem without writing code or having specialized data-science training. The idea is to democratize these learning methods and models to everyone in the organization, producing dynamic results that can be acted upon.

This journey won't happen overnight. Start now, and start small, sparking insights throughout your organization

---

16   Jeremy Herman and Mike Del Blaso, "Meet Michelangelo: Uber's Machine Learning Platform," *Uber Engineering,* September 5, 2017, https://eng.uber.com/michelangelo/.

with a dynamic data dashboard. Once that is done, you can start figuring out how to democratize predictive capabilities with a machine-intelligence platform to enhance everyone's decision-making.

PRINCIPLE FIVE: DATA SCIENCE VALUE AS A KEY PERFORMANCE INDICATOR (KPI)

The fifth principle is all about taking action. You must measure the value and impact of data science and machine learning on your business and make this metric one of your key performance indicators (KPI). Always start with a small machine-intelligence initiative and investment, measure its success, demonstrate ROI, and then take on larger initiatives, while celebrating the wins and democratizing the knowledge throughout your organization.

In doing this, prioritize data-science investments with the highest potential ROI. A typical chief information or chief data officer at a Fortune 50 or Fortune 200 company receives more than 2,000 to 2,500 requests a year for different data products. People within the organization think they should act upon all these, which is rarely feasible.

How should you prioritize? Look at an investment's feasibility and impact. Feasibility refers to whether you have the data or not. Is the data clean and labeled? Do you have the talent, resources, and processes to get the project started? Impact refers to financial contribution. If you're going to invest in this project, will it genuinely revolutionize your business over time? Will it add millions of dollars, or will it add $10,000?

In a graph where the x axis is feasibility, and the y axis is impact, you want to start with a target at the top-right corner: high feasibility and high impact. Start with what will help you transform your organization immediately, and as you mature, move on to projects that still have high feasibility and perhaps less impact but that will also be able to push the organization forward.

Think about these two dimensions before you submit a request to your CIO for a project you think might be a good use case. Particularly when starting the journey, you don't want everyone to submit hundreds of use cases. You want to grab one with high feasibility and impact that will be able to transform your organization quickly.

Starting small can be aligned with getting maximum impact. Most people think you need to invest millions of dollars in data-science projects to see millions of dollars in added value. That's not true. If you choose projects with high feasibility and high impact, you don't need to spend millions. You can start small. You don't need to pour $5 million into the project and hire 250 people. Instead, begin with a small investment, get a few people to start the project, see if it works, measure ROI, and decide if it adds value to the company. If so, expand and put more money into it while celebrating the win.

Data-science and machine-intelligence projects that can revolutionize and transform your organization don't need to be expensive. In fact, you have to start small because you must test your hypothesis to see if it moves the needle. Start by piloting a project. If you see that a magnitude of change is reasonable, pour more money into it: invest more and hire more. Then operationalize it throughout the organization.

PRINCIPLE 6: DATA GOVERNANCE

This principle is all about the environment in which your data sits. Your data assets must be secure and private. This is a priority, and all large corporations should have thoroughly established data governance, security, and privacy by this time. By my standards, however, many of the companies I work with are still quite far behind the curve. While the importance of safeguards should go without saying, it still needs to be said: many organizations haven't yet instituted them.

This is a Pandora's box that could kill an entire organization, as recent events have demonstrated.[17] Think

---

17 Matthew Rosenberg, "How Trump Consultants Exploited the Facebook Data of Millions," New York *Times*, March 3, 2018, https://www.nytimes.com/2018/03/17/us/politics/cambridge-analytica-trump-campaign.html.

about the repercussions. Humans, not machines, are responsible for data governance. Other people in the organization often treat those responsible for data governance like black sheep because they protect data. This is unacceptable. Security is a key principle in a data- and model-driven enterprise. It creates a healthy environment. However, as machines (rather than people) start becoming data-security gatekeepers, it's possible that much of the anxiety and anger people now feel toward data-governance teams will dissipate. You'll find a concrete example of this in the case studies in Part 3.

SUMMARY: DATA-DRIVEN MATURITY HORIZONS

By way of summary, how can you tell if you're applying these principles properly and effectively? I call the chronological stages companies go through to become data-driven the four "maturity horizons." This is a gradual but critical process.

The *first stage* is to start with yourself, asking not what you think but what you know. When you ask your reports, "What do you know?" "What do you have?" and "Where's the data?" they'll follow suit. They'll also stop relying on gut feelings and start asking, "What do I know?" When you change your habits, you change the habits of the people that report to you.

Positive transformations should start with you because they will trickle throughout the organization. You are a role model people look up to. If you start a journey, other people will join you.

The *second stage* is to start maximizing benefits from the data you already have. Stop shopping around for data elsewhere or finding excuses for why you don't have "enough data" or "the right data." You already have a lot of data. Focus on that. Create a strategy for how to leverage and maximize its benefits. You'd be surprised by how much gold you already have access to. You're not dependent on anyone else's contributions. Start with what you have, and you'll be astonished to find how many insights and gemstones you can extract from existing data.

The *third stage* of data maturity is to start promoting the utilization of data throughout the organization. This relates to the principle that in order to democratize data, you need to have the metadata that allows people to access it. Then start value-added data initiatives, promote them, and show other teams and people within the organization how data science and machine intelligence can transform your business. When people see live showcases of how you can leverage data with modeling techniques, they will follow suit because they'll want to build out their own verticals.

Again, this is about celebrating victories. Organizations today are not good at celebrating and sharing wins when it comes to machine-intelligence capabilities. They create projects that implement machine intelligence, but they don't democratize the knowledge or promote the utilization of the data or modeling techniques they have created throughout the organization.

One thing expected from twenty-first-century business leaders is, if you created the model for one use case, can you replicate it in other verticals within the business? Promoting utilization of data and modeling techniques can create synergy, with the organization bridging data and modeling techniques horizontally across various groups and "silos."

The *fourth stage* of data maturity is building a company-wide data platform, like Airbnb and Uber have, to which everyone contributes. Everyone has access to the company's metadata and can have access to the data itself as appropriate or necessary. This facilitates a greater and greater number of actionable opportunities to utilize machine-intelligence techniques.

This last stage is about leveraging data. Horizontally, you already have deeply embedded machine-intelligence capabilities in the organization. Everyone makes data-driven decisions and moves toward predictive rather than descriptive types of analysis. This is when your enterprise is truly data-driven.

The journey won't happen overnight. You always need to start with yourself: with your habits and your way of thinking, with hard work and deep intention (as I learned in my own yoga practice) the rest will follow.

PART II

DATA-SCIENCE WORKFLOW AND CHANGE MANAGEMENT

CHAPTER 5

AN EXECUTIVE PERSPECTIVE ON DATA-SCIENCE WORKFLOW

Business leaders need to understand data-science workflow to better communicate with both technical and non-technical teams and develop critical thinking about each of the workflow's phases. When outcomes or predictions arrive on your desk, you need to know how to evaluate them: how to critique recommendations, ask the right questions, and ensure that the analyses and project are headed in the right direction, aligned with your ROI goals.

The idea here isn't to turn you into a data scientist or train you in depth in data-science concepts and techniques. Rather, the purpose is to help you develop a data literacy and mindset capable of critiquing and validating data scientists' work and machine-intelligence recommendations.

A major gap being faced in the Fourth Industrial Revolution is business leaders' lack of knowledge about what and how data science and machine learning work. One way of closing this gap is to guide you, as a business leader, through the data-science workflow so you have a better understanding of what it entails.

It's important to realize that this workflow involves both technical and non-technical teams. When you embark on the journey to become a data- and model-driven enterprise, you need to think about the end-to-end change management this workflow will require right from the very beginning.

Business leaders and non-technical teams play major roles in the data-science workflow, just as data scientists, engineers, and technical teams do. Once you understand this, you'll be able to tailor and implement the change management required to operationalize data-science projects within your organization and its specific cultural constraints.

There are four major phases in the data-science workflow:

ask, acquire, analyze, and **act**. This chapter will give an overview of these phases, while each of the following four chapters in Part 2 will examine the steps in each phase in greater depth.

Ask relates to the initial phase or starting point of embarking on a project. Executives must first identify business problems and ask great questions that data and modeling techniques can answer.

Acquire is the second phase in the business workflow but also the first phase that truly involves data-science technology. After you identify a business problem that can be translated into a data problem, you need to embark on a discovery phase: What data do you have? What does it tell you? Data scientists call this phase exploratory data analysis (EDA). You then need to prepare the data for production. Data scientists call this "standardizing the data" or normalizing it so it can be input into the model. As previously mentioned, this often involves labeling and structuring the data.

In the third phase, **analyze**, machine intelligence models are applied to and transform the data to gain insights and generate predictive power. You, as a business leader, will then evaluate the resulting output, outcomes, and recommendations. In this phase, executives need to know how to critique the results and recommendations their technical team brings to the table. Are they reliable? Have they been properly vetted? Are these predications I can choose among and act on? The case studies later in the book will help you develop and hone these critical skills.

The fourth phase is **act**. I always emphasize that machine-intelligence models by themselves do not add value. Of course, you will have hired smart technical people to prepare the data and create the models to analyze it properly. However, these models and their output will not by themselves add any value to your organization.

Value will be added only when you decide which recommendation to act on, and then not only act on it but operationalize it throughout your organization. This is one of the largest barriers and gaps in the industries right now: companies do not act on machine-intelligence output and therefore cannot realize related ROI. The current change-management structure is broken and inadequate to the needs of the Fourth Industrial Revolution.

As an executive, you first need to interpret results to ensure they're meaningful and aligned with your intuition. Then you must institute the change management necessary to operationalize the benefits of your machine-intelligence investment and enhance your overall decision-making process.

To summarize, start with *asking* interesting questions about how your data can be used. Have your technical team *acquire* and prepare the data. Then *analyze* it, first by having your technical team create and apply machine-intelligence models, and then evaluating the results yourself. Finally, *act* to operationalize these data-science models so they can add value to your organization. Then measure ROI and reinvest. In the meantime, don't forget to celebrate wins!

There are ten steps within these phases, as illustrated in the following diagram.

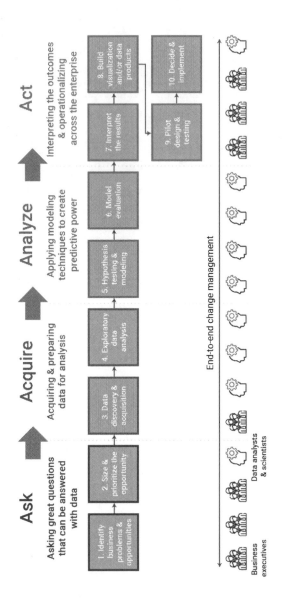

We'll now go on to look at the steps in each of these phases, and then deal with the all-important issue of change management, which affects all the phases and steps.

CHAPTER 6

ASK PHASE AND STEPS

Ask

Asking great quesions
that can be answered
with data

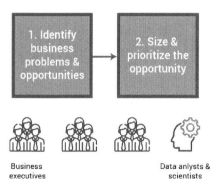

Ask, the first phase, involves asking great questions
aligned with your business objectives to which data can

spark an answer. The current gap is in the ability to translate business problems into solvable data and modeling techniques. As mentioned earlier, without any specific guidance or additional education, executives generally say 75 percent of their top business problems can be solved with the data their organization already has access to. But with more knowledge, awareness, and experience of the capabilities of data science and machine learning, this percentage will be much higher: close to 100 percent.

In the data-driven, model-driven world of the Fourth Industrial Revolution, all business decisions can and should be solved by leveraging data and modeling techniques. This is done by asking interesting business questions that:

- Correlate with your organization's goals
- Generate ROI and provide valuable experience
- Acquire more leads and clients
- Allow you to interact with your users more effectively
- Deepen and revolutionize your organization's competitive advantage

Asking smart questions—high-level rather than niche questions—that can push the organization forward is the central theme of this first phase. The focus here is on executives and business rather than technical teams.

There are two steps in the ask phase.

1. Identify business problems & opportunities

The **first step** is to translate crucial business problems into data opportunities. In workshops, I ask executives to write down their top five business problems and think about how these can be solved by leveraging data their organizations already have with modeling techniques. Think about interesting case studies with extremely high visibility and high business impact. Choose cases where you can move the needle and push your organization forward: cases that can revolutionize your business.

These business problems must then be turned into problems that can be solved with the application of data and modeling techniques. Some experience may be required to do so, as this step is not always intuitive. Translating business problems into data and modeling solutions takes time and exposure to different business problems and modeling techniques. With time, you'll develop a machine-intelligence mindset that will help you translate your business problems into data problems more intuitively. One way to get started is to familiarize yourself with the different modeling techniques that will be described in the case studies.

You, as an executive, must learn to turn business problems you are already familiar with into use cases that, by leveraging data and modeling techniques, can revolutionize your business. In time, by developing data literacy and a machine-intelligence mindset, you will learn how to do this efficiently and effectively. That is the purpose of the case studies later in the book: they'll help you spark and develop your intuition on the relationship between business problems and learning models so that you can start applying this knowledge to your organization's real-life issues.

2. Size & prioritize the opportunity

At this point, you're a business leader who has identified a business opportunity. But before embarking on an analysis, you must first prioritize the opportunity you've identified, making sure you're embarking on a journey with use cases that will move the needle. This is the **second step** in the ask phase.

Ask yourself, "What is the back of the envelope ROI calculation for this project?" For example, what will the potential impact on your business of identifying more creditworthy applications be in the first, second, and third years? Identify the revenue uplift that might result. How revolutionary will this model's business impact be? In the case studies, you'll see examples of how back-of-the-envelope calculations can determine the potential ROI of machine-intelligence initiatives that are both intuitive and as accurate as possible.

There is another imperative in the ask phase. You must start thinking—right at the beginning—about the change-management process this initiative will eventually require. This is a crucial point that will be discussed in the next chapter. When you have a working data product that demonstrates the estimated ROI, how are you going to operationalize it, creating a seamless change management process that will integrate this solution and its benefits within your business environment and your employees' daily workflow?

CHAPTER 7

ACQUIRE PHASE AND STEPS

Acquire

Acquiring & preparing
data for analysis

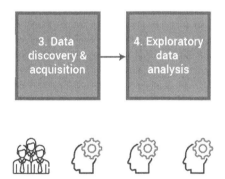

Acquire, the workflow's second phase, involves acquiring
and preparing data for analysis and modeling.

3. Data discovery & acquisition

In the first step of this phase and **third step** of the entire workflow, you—or rather, your technical team—acquire and process raw data, labeling, normalizing, and standardizing it as needed to be input into your learning model. As this proceeds, you will become more familiar with and able to validate your data. You can make sure you have enough data and that it is aligned with your intuition of how to solve your business problem before embarking on creating your model.

The main task in this step is to explore the data you already have and shape it so it can be input into your models. This is the time when you want to partner with different departments and verticals within your organization, gathering the relevant data, making sure that it is in the right shape—for example, labeled correctly—and that you have the necessary documentation.

4. Exploratory data analysis

The second step of the acquire phase—the **fourth step** of the overall workflow—is having the technical team do an exploratory data analysis (EDA). During this step, the technical team, with your help, will work on validating your hypotheses and intuitions, and see if the data contains any anomalies or outliers.

At this point, you on the business side will be better equipped to determine if your intuitive hypotheses are valid. As you proceed, you will often discover new trends and anomalies that go beyond what your intuition originally told you.

Once an EDA helps you better familiarize yourself with the data, you will see, with the help of your technical team, if there are any data outliers that could skew the analysis. If so, alterations must be made. The EDA will help both the technical and non-technical teams determine if you have the right data to answer the initial business question. Is the data in the right shape? Is it labeled? Do we need more data to answer this critical question? This stage will also help you figure out if you need to refine your initial business question.

During this step, the technical team does feature engineering, which means throwing a lot of variables and features at the model, which enables it to learn, better recognize patterns, and determine which of these variables and features are most important for the analysis. Again, we don't want to overfit or be too specific in the analysis. If the analysis involves too many features, the chances of overfitting increases. Pick a smaller, more optimal subset that can better explain the y target.

CHAPTER 8

ANALYZE PHASE AND STEPS

Analyze

Applying modeling techniques to create predictive power

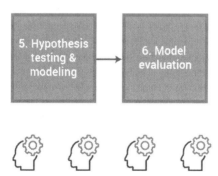

The third phase, **analyze**, is the hard-core modeling phase in the data-science journey, one you want highly technical data scientists to focus on. The technical team applies different modeling techniques that will help you understand the trends and insights the data implies.

This will be the most technical chapter in the book. Business leaders do not need to learn the technical details of the modeling and evaluative techniques covered here. However, you do need to know enough about this phase to be able to understand and critique results. What's important are the concepts, not the details, and the case studies in Part 3 have been included to help reinforce and apply the conceptual material presented here.

However, if you are interested in learning a bit more technical detail about the three main classes of machine-learning algorithms—supervised learning, unsupervised learning, and semi-supervised learning—please turn to Appendix B, which will give you an overview.

Let's begin with an important definition. A data-science model or modeling technique can be statistical, mathematical, or involve machine learning. With curated data, models can discern patterns and provide you with output that has predictive power of some kind, providing an explanation of the issue under investigation: the y target or goal of the analysis, whether observed or not.

These modeling techniques try to predict and describe the y, which is also known as the dependent variable, since it depends on the model's x input. Modeling techniques shed light on what features can contribute to and explain y, for example, what might cause a customer to buy an iPhone.

In the first step of this phase—the **fifth step** of the overall workflow—a few different models are chosen and employed to validate which one is best able to solve your initial business problem and meet your goals. This is critical: there's no single "winning horse" or single model that can explain everything. A few different models must always be chosen and tested. Three examples of such models are **random forest, logistic regression**, and **neural networks**. These of course are only three of a myriad of modeling techniques, with more being developed all the time.

Please note, if you wish, you can find a somewhat more technical description of these models and other machine-learning techniques in this chapter's sidebars.

RANDOM FOREST

A random forest model is a type of decision tree that runs different scenarios to determine how to generate the right output. "Random forest" basically explores the different paths data takes over time and can help you understand why a decision was made by assembling a number of decision trees to find the one that best explains, for example, why a customer might default on an unsecured loan. In a decision tree, you look at whether A input leads to B or C outcome, and so forth.

LOGISTIC REGRESSION

A logistic regression model is a regression analysis used when the dependent variable (outcome) is binary, such as yes/no or pass/fail. It is a so-called bounded function, which means it will always generate results between zero and one. Say a bank is looking at whether a customer will default on a loan. The higher the number produced by the logistic regression model, the higher the probability the customer will default.

NEURAL NETWORKS

A "deep-learning" neural network is a machine-intelligence model that inspired by the biological neural networks that constitute the animal brain. These models have an input layer, an output layer, and a variety of hidden layers in between that simulate the way data flows between the different layers of neurons in our brains. These models typically generate predictions that tightly fit the input data and have formidable predictive power.

Neural networks' downside, however, is that they can be computationally expensive because they allow data to flow in so many different, often indirect, directions. Nor do we necessarily know how to trace how the data flows through these complicated layers, which means it's difficult—and also often unnecessary—to determine exactly how the models generate outcomes, which is why a deep-learning neural network is often thought of as a black box.

6. Model evaluation

In the second step of this phase—the **sixth step** of the overall workflow—the results the different models yield are benchmarked using several different evaluation techniques. This benchmarking enables you to choose the model that best fits the data and demonstrates high performance with respect to the metrics you have determined the analysis must yield.

Sometimes this phase can reveal interesting results you wouldn't have expected, because machine-intelligence models think differently than we do. A model can crunch millions of data points in an egalitarian way. There's quite a lot to learn from the process of interpreting these results, and you, as a business leader, must invest time and energy doing so.

Data scientists have different measures of fit and performance, and through testing and benchmarking, can determine which are the best for the problem at hand. As an executive, it's essential for you to understand these performance metrics so you can critique the results that data scientists bring you once this phase is complete. A number of these modeling and evaluation techniques will be demonstrated in the case studies in Part 3.

In recent years, with the advent of deep-learning neural networks, everyone has come to believe that these complex models are very sexy—because they are! However, you don't always need to use an extremely sophisticated learning algorithm such as a neural network. Why not? Because they're costly, complex, and require labeled data and a lot of computational power.

A basic algorithm can, in some cases, produce better results than fancy, complex ones. So don't jump straight to fancy, complex, and expensive analyses. Easier, simpler, statistical learning models can still solve big problems. Start with something modest and simple, validate the results, measure the ROI, and reevaluate your strategic investment.

As part of this analysis, data scientists typically take an entire data set and split it randomly into training and validation (or testing) data. The training set is the subset of the original data that the model is trained with. The training data set tunes the model's parameters, and any residual or anomalous data is set aside.

Imagine you have a container that represents your entire data set. Half of what's in the container will be chosen randomly to train and tune the model. The other half of the data in the container is the validation set: the second data subset. Partitioning can also be used to obtain more randomized subsets. After the model has been trained with the first data subset, you imitate a real-world scenario in which new data flows into the model. You then validate how well the trained model performs on this new data. You feed the validation data set into the model to determine if the results you originally obtained and the parameters you originally created still hold. If not, you tweak them. This technique is known as **cross-validation**.

As previously mentioned, you don't want the model to be too specifically fitted to the training data. The model must be generalized enough so that when new data is input, the model still holds. The data input into the model shouldn't need to be too similar to the training data for the model to perform accurately. The training data set will train the model's initial parameters, and the validation data set ensures that when new data is input, it doesn't need to be in the exact same shape as the original training data. Given the wealth of data we deal with in the real world now, we can't define our data sets too narrowly.

In other words, we don't want **overfitting**. By the same token, we don't want **underfitting**, in which the relationship between the data and model is too loose and the model's predictive power is low.

EVALUATION TECHNIQUES: CROSS-VALIDATION

The idea here is to split the data into two parts. One is training data: the data used to train the model. We can then test the model on the data that wasn't included in the training phase. Remember, machine-learning models are OODA loops. This is an iterative process, and every time you go through the loop, inputting new data generated by the model's most recent output, the process is refined, and predictive power increases.

This new input is part of the test data set and is meant to replicate and refine what happened in the training-data process. The model ingests the new data, and the new output will ultimately be added to the original data set. When new data is input, it's important to ensure that the model's predictions still hold. The model must be generalized enough for predictions to remain accurate when different data sets are input.

OVERFITTING AND UNDERFITTING

Is your model accurate 100 percent of the time? In machine learning, perfection can be a fault rather than a virtue. When I see a model with close to 100 percent accuracy, I worry, because this might indicate the model is overfitting the training data. When new data enters the model, it might generate incorrect predictions.

One hundred percent accuracy might also indicate that we're overfitting for trends and patterns in a specific training data set. In an iterative loop, new data will be input, meaning models must be generalized enough and not too specific.

But you can't underfit either. You don't want a generic, overly relaxed model that doesn't fit the data well. The predictions generated in the training data set must be highly, although not 100 percent, accurate.

The right balance between underfitting and overfitting will generate predictions that describe and analyze the data efficiently. When new data is input, the model's predictions will continue to hold.

These principles are illustrated in the following graphic.

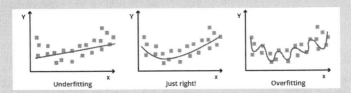

Precision and recall are better measures of predictive power than accuracy, but there are some trade-offs and pitfalls to pay attention to in both cases. When considering how precise our predictions are in comparison to the training or observed data set, higher levels of precision mean the model will miss some cases.

Other techniques for model evaluation include the **confusion metric, accuracy,** and the two interrelated factors of **precision** and **recall.** All will reoccur in the case studies in Part 3.

EVALUATION TECHNIQUES: CONFUSION METRIC

The confusion metric, one of the most important evaluation techniques, is a table showing the number of predictions for each class compared to the number of instances that previous observation tells us really belong to that class. In comparing the predictive class with the observed data, we are basically looking at and comparing true negatives and true positives.

Specifically, one side of the table gives the observed class, the data we already know to be true. This is the data we originally input into the model, which is deterministic and has no uncertainty, as it reflects events that have already occurred. On the other side of the table are the non-deterministic predictions and outcomes the model generates.

Here's an example of a confusion-metric table.

		Predicted Class	
		No	Yes
Observed Class	No	TN	FP
	Yes	FN	TP

TN	True Negative
FP	False Positive
FN	False Negative
TP	True Positive

This comparison of the different elements in the table helps you obtain a general overview of the types of mistakes the machine-intelligence algorithm makes. The confusion metric can show us the model's accuracy, its true positives, its false positives, and its measures of sensitivity and specificity.

EVALUATION TECHNIQUES: ACCURACY

Accuracy is another important evaluation technique that determines how often the model got it right. For example, how good is the model at simultaneously identifying both sick and healthy people? Accuracy is both an interesting and simple evaluation technique, yielding the percentage of exactly how accurate the model is. However, it also comes with pitfalls.

But what does 100 percent accuracy mean? Is 100 percent accuracy a good thing? Should we rely on any analysis that yields 100 percent accuracy? As mentioned elsewhere, the answer is no. When you see a very high accuracy level, this typically means that the model overfits the data: it's not generalized enough. The model has been tuned by overfitting the training data.

Therefore, when new data is input, the model will underperform because the data will be different. The model's performance and results won't be accurate enough. You want neither **underfitting**, in which the model is too generalized and the outcomes therefore uninformative, nor **overfitting**, in which the model is too specific. It's better to have something in the middle. That way, the model will include good representations of both its analytic parameters and the data. When new data is analyzed, the model will still hold.

EVALUATION TECHNIQUES:
PRECISION AND RECALL

Precision and recall are two important, related measures of performance fit. Precision refers to how useful and relevant information is. It is the ratio of correctly predicted positive values to the total number of predicted positive values, whether correct or not. This metric highlights the percentage of correct positive predictions to all positive predictions. High precision yields a low "false positive" rate.

Think about someone manually investigating credit applications and identifying those that may potentially lead to fraud. He wants to be as precise—to make as few mistakes—as possible since he wants to prevent possible fraud. He wants to identify all the real fraud cases out of those that might be fraudulent with great precision. His target is narrow because he doesn't want to miss anything. If something is missed, it will be costly.

The second, complementary measure is recall. Recall is the ratio of correctly predicted positive values to actual positive values. Recall highlights the sensitivity of the model: how many, out of all actual positives, did the model catch?

In our example, recall identifies the percentage of all potentially fraudulent cases that can be identified as actual fraud. An individual managing a financial institution's overall risk would be interested in the recall metric in this case. She needs to have as wide a perspective as possible. She needs high recall because when assessing and measuring a bank's overall risk, she wants her analysis to encompass all cases globally. In this scenario, a model will input all cases represented by the data and use the majority to make a prediction.

A good model will encompass both precision and recall, balancing the two factors, because you don't want to be too narrow or too wide. Again, there's a trade-off. If you're too wide—if there is too much recall—the analysis will not provide high accuracy. If you're too narrow, you might miss data that can shed light on the goal of the analysis, such as the trustworthiness of the customers who have applied for loans.

There are many other mathematical and statistical model-evaluation techniques with names like the **Receiver Operating Characteristic Curve (ROC Curve), Gini Coefficient,** and **Root Mean Squared Error (RMSE).** The idea here is that you don't need to become an expert in how these model-evaluation techniques work from a mathematical or statistical perspective. You just need a general understanding of what they mean and how to interpret them. What's the bottom line? This may be somewhat different for each analysis.

RECEIVER OPERATING CHARACTERISTIC CURVE (ROC CURVE)

ROC curves calculate the extent to which any predictive model can distinguish between true positions and true negatives. A model needs to predict both a positive as a positive and a negative as a negative. ROC curves plot sensitivity, the probability of predicting that a real positive will be identified as a positive, as well as 1-specificity, the probability of predicting that a real negative will be identified as a negative.

GINI COEFFICIENT

The Gini coefficient—named after Italian statistician Corrado Gini—measures the equality or inequality among values along a distribution curve, such as a curve showing distribution or levels of income. It is another bounded function whose results are between zero and one. A Gini coefficient of zero indicates perfect equality. All values along the distribution curve are the same, which would be the case, for example, if everyone sampled had the same income. By contrast, a Gini coefficient of one indicates 100 percent inequality. If one person among all those sampled had all the income and the others had none, the Gini coefficient would approach one.

ROOT MEAN SQUARE ERROR (RMSE)

RMSE is a measure of the average number of errors a model makes. You don't need to know how this measure is arrived at, but you do need to know whether you want a high or low RMSE. Since RMSE represents the average number of errors a model generates, you will generally want a low RMSE.

CHAPTER 9

—

ACT PHASE
AND STEPS

Act

Interpreting the outcomes
& operationalizing
across the enterprise

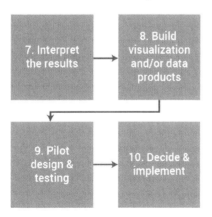

The fourth phase of the data science workflow, **act,** is the most important. It really can't be said too often: models by themselves will not add value if business leaders don't know how to interpret their outcomes and understand how to act to operationalize them across the enterprise. Otherwise, your business will not realize ROI from its data-science initiatives.

Once pilot tests demonstrate good results and ROI, make decisions based on what you've learned. Act! Operationalize the process in your organization, making sure the tested models are highly embedded in the daily routine of people making those business decisions.

7. Interpret the results

The first step of the act phase—the **seventh step** of the overall data-science workflow—is to evaluate the results or output of your machine-intelligence models. In this step we move back from the data and technical side to the business side of the equation. In the previous step, we benchmarked results from our models with the methods mentioned above, as well as others that will appear in the case studies.

In step 7, you want to learn from the results to inform product offerings, strategies, and correct implementation. You interpret the results from the models, make sure they are aligned with your intuition, and figure out what can you can do to solve the initial business problem based on this knowledge.

8. Build visualization and/or data products

Data visualization, the second step in the act phase—and **step 8** in the overall workflow—is critical to proper interpretation and evaluation. The difference between good data scientists and great data scientists is their ability to do data visualization. Every data scientist can code, but not every data scientist knows how to communicate the results of these models efficiently, effectively, and artistically.

Even with smart, sophisticated models, business leaders will only be able to understand the results if they are presented artistically in a way that resonates like a good story would. Data visualization is all about telling the story behind the data. If people in the organization don't understand the story behind the data, the results won't affect decision-making, which is the entire purpose of the data-science workflow.

Therefore, data visualization is a large component of data science, and people need to invest time in developing artistic ways to take raw numbers and present them in a way that allows everyone in the organization to grasp and understand what they mean.

9. Pilot design & testing

The third step in the act phase—the **ninth step** in the overall workflow—is to test the models, pilot them, and demonstrate ROI. Once you pilot a model in a real-world setting, your organization can start incorporating the model's predictions into decision-making, which means you'll be able to measure the project's ROI more accurately. You'll be able to see what the increase in revenue is, how many more clients you have, or how much more efficient your organization is. Once you take the crucial step of demonstrating ROI, I urge you to celebrate your success across the organization. Most businesses aren't very good at this and need to get better! You can also determine if you want to expand the initiative by making further investments.

10. Decide &
implement

The fourth step in the act phase—the **tenth and final step** overall—is about operationalizing machine-intelligence models to enhance decision-making. This is the step that transforms your business into a data-driven organization. Often, this requires creating short-, medium-, and long-term strategies until the models are fully embedded. After you create a model, it will take some time to operationalize it fully in the system. But don't wait to begin reaping the benefits.

It's perfectly fine to do some manual work in the beginning while continuing to get dynamic input from your machine-intelligence models. Sometimes it makes sense to go through predictions one by one and to see how the results align with some of your other, older methods, to start moving the organization forward. First figure out your short-term strategy and then your long-term strategy for operationalizing the model. Don't give up!

Businesses currently don't implement or abandon about 60 percent of their analytics projects. because executives don't think about these short-term strategies for implementation. Most often a system enhancement, new process, culture shift, and talent acquisition are the barriers to successful implementation when and if you do not think about these aspects very early on in the process. This means that the organization cannot benefit from the models that have been created and tested in either the short or the long term. The case studies in Part 3 will show you how to think about finding short-term solutions that can start leveraging modeling techniques immediately.

IN SUMMARY

The above description of the ten generic, high-level steps in the data-science workflow has been intended to expose you to a mindset: to show you what data scientists and technical teams do at each phase of this workflow journey and to demonstrate that the workflow involves technical and non-technical teams working together to seize opportunities and realize ROI.

Along the way, be prepared to learn through an iterative process of trial and error, just as machine-intelligence models do. There is no single winning horse, no model you can be sure is the right one before it is tested.

I have learned—thanks, Shachar—that "everything we do is wrong, but it's always better to be wrong and strong than wrong and weak." By leveraging data, you are strong even if you are wrong, that is, if you have picked the wrong model. If you only go on gut feeling, you're being wrong and weak. Machine-intelligence models try to imitate life, but no one can predict the future with 100 percent accuracy. We live in a probabilistic and uncertain world. In learning from past data and trends, machine-intelligence models take account of and even imitate this uncertainty.

The point is that some models will yield greater accuracy than others when addressing specific business problems. The case studies in the third part of this book will give you techniques for determining which model best fits your business problem and the associated data.

CHAPTER 10

―――

CHANGE MANAGEMENT: THE VITAL STEP

Change management is the vital step in operationalizing data-science projects and transforming your organization into a data- and model-driven enterprise. I've learned in working closely with large enterprises that about 60 percent of data-science initiatives never get fully implemented because business leaders do not pay attention to crucial change-management processes that need to be considered from the very beginning. If you don't think about how to operationalize machine-intelligence at the start of a project, you won't be able to transform your business or realize ROI.

Here are some reasons why organizations are currently

failing to implement machine-intelligence models due to broken change management:

1. **System Integration:** System adoption and enhancement takes time. To implement a project, an enterprise must start working with their IT team and software vendors typically eight months prior to implementation.

2. **Fulfilment:** Enterprises often haven't organized and connected teams to successfully fulfill offers based on predictions from their models as early as necessary.

3. **Feedback Loop:** Organizations in which technical and business teams do not collaborate miss the opportunity to create a feedback loop. This flattens a machine-intelligence models' learning curve, resulting in the generating low-quality offers to customers.

4. **Organizational Roles:** Organizations fail to put technical employees in a position where they can influence and implement machine-learning projects, even after they have gone through training and upskilling and have launched data-science and machine-learning projects ready to add proven value to the business.

Business leaders should become familiar with the data-science workflow, particularly the personas involved in each phase, and determine how and when to enter a new style of change management that will ensure successful implementation of machine-intelligence models. Without agile change management, your organization will not be able to seize opportunities and realize all the initiative's potential ROI.

Why is change management the vital step? Most of the executives I speak with have been trained at an Ivy League or similar institution in the United States or abroad. Unfortunately, when they went to Harvard, Berkeley, Wharton, or one of the other great business schools, they were trained in an old-fashioned change-management process in which most project decisions were business-led and led almost exclusively by non-technical people.

In the twenty-first century, change management involves more than business leaders and executives. Technical people now have a prominent and integral role in the process. Fourth Industrial Revolution change-management processes involve both business *and* technical teams.

This unaccustomed shift in perspective feels foreign to business leaders. You haven't been trained to think like this or to determine the steps necessary to create a process that operates seamlessly between business and technical teams. Most non-technical business leaders are not familiar with technical personas, their vocabulary, or their way of working. Realizing the ROI from implementation of machine-intelligence models requires a proverbial paradigm shift.

It's up to you, the executive, to decide how to act on the insights machine intelligence generates. You must also figure out the short-, medium-, and long-term strategies for implementing these models within the organization. In the past, upper-echelon members of the business team led change management. Today, highly involved technical people co-lead it. You have non-technical people, such as business leaders and executives, and technical people, like engineers and data scientists, as parts of a unified team tasked with efficiently designing and operationalizing business projects.

COLLABORATION: WHO DOES WHAT

In the data-science workflow, you need to start figuring out early on how to create a process where technical and non-technical teams can work together because, as you can see, this workflow incorporates a fusion of these two very different personas.

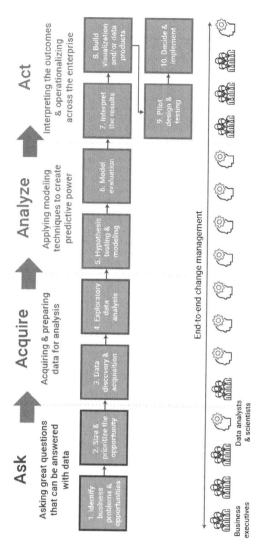

Both business and technical teams are critical parts of the change-management process. One of the biggest gaps in the Fourth Industrial Revolution is that between technical and non-technical teams. How can we bring them closer together so they work hand in hand?

Part of this involves determining and understanding who does what. Business executives lead certain parts of the process; technical teams lead other parts. To become a data- and model-driven enterprise, you need to figure out how to bring the two teams together to respond as quickly and nimbly as possible to rapidly evolving trends in machine intelligence.

To do so, first clearly define who leads each phase of the workflow. If you test and redefine this iteratively, your organization will soon develop a workflow that allows rapid implementation of machine-intelligence models.

In general, the first stage—ask—involves the business team asking great questions. The second stage—acquire—in which data prepared the analysis, involves a combination of technical and non-technical teams. The third stage—analysis—where modeling techniques leverage the data to create predictive power, principally involves the engineers in your technical team. The final stage—act—involves both business leaders and engineers working to interpret, through an operational lens, the results these models generate.

However, creating a synergistic workflow between business and technical teams in your particular enterprise will be an iterative process. Some change-management decisions will be better than others, but over time, things will continue to improve and begin working more smoothly.

SAMPLE COLLABORATIVE WORKFLOW

This workflow will be specific to each business: no one size will fit all. However, by way of example, consider the following generic workflow:

At the top of this graphic, at position number 1, are predictions generated by the technical team. This is the first step in the representative workflow. The second step is for the business team to determine, based on these predictions, what a product's value proposition will be for each client or user. Then, as the third step, the business team must decide, based on output from its machine-intelligence models, which tailored messages to deliver to which audiences to convey that value proposition.

Before sending these messages, in step 4, the technical team collects data to determine which channels will most effectively relay these messages to each type of user. How did the customers you targeted through different channels engage with those messages? This data will come from past interactions, like email and social media. In this phase, the technical team aggregates data and determines how best to input it into machine-intelligence models, with the output shedding light on how to interact with your customers. Once offers are made and accepted, it's up to the business team to determine—in step 5—how to fulfill those offers.

The technical team becomes involved again in step 6, tracking whether an offer has been fulfilled and whether and how the customer is engaging with the product. How much money has been spent? What interactions have taken place? Once tracked, all this new data can be plugged in to the model to enhance its performance and future output. Refining the model and generating better results depend on iteratively feeding it the latest data.

After customers engage with the product, you can learn what works, what doesn't, and how you can keep improving. You get dynamic insight into your customers' preferences. In step 7, the business team determines how to improve the company's products and offerings. You now return to step 1, in which the technical team makes predictions about the impact these changes will have. The cycle has come full circle and can be repeated ad infinitum.

LESSONS LEARNED

What's most critical here is obviously the synergy between your business and technical teams. Of course, every organization has its own culture and processes, and this example is therefore generic.

This feedback loop continues indefinitely, and over time, your machine-intelligence models continue to learn because they are constantly receiving new data. The business team is also learning and evolving because it's receiving data and feedback that can help improve the company's products and services.

Some changes will be business-led. Some will be technology-led. The point is that overall operational change management involves both business and technical teams.

New processes involving improved, closer communication between technical and non-technical people are needed. The teams must learn how to work together, and you, as a business leader, must figure out how to create a culture and environment that enables this. Education and possible changes in organizational structure can help bridge the gap between the two teams.

ONE STEP FORWARD

In Chapter 4, the role of a semi-technical "middleman"/ "middlewoman" —who stands between the technical and business teams and helps them understand one another— was mentioned. Let's look at this and related roles more closely, as they can greatly facilitate change management.

First, look at the different roles within a technical team. Data scientists are paid a lot of money. This means they should be focused on hard-core data modeling, the most crucial, brain-draining aspect of the job, and the reason they're paid so much.

Instead, in many companies, data scientists are often made to focus on low-hanging fruit, like labeling, normalizing, and ensuring data can be properly input into learning models. This is a job for a different persona, the data analyst, a necessary role but one that adds less value than the data scientist, who should focus on the models themselves.

With additional training, a data analyst may also be a

good fit for the role of the middleman or semi-technical person who understands both the business problems and technical issues involved. Some companies call this person a **data translator**. Whatever the name, this role is that of facilitator: someone who holds the technical team's hand on one side, and the non-technical team's on the other, bridging the gap between the two.

This is a cutting-edge topic. You can expect the role of data translator or semitechnical middleman to grow exponentially in the coming years as companies realize the urgent need to close the gap between technical and non-technical teams. We already see many companies upskilling their current workforce and training some non-technical people to become semitechnical.

The people filling this role understand the business side and the rationale behind business problems and why the organization wants to embark on a data-science or machine-intelligence journey to solve those problems. They know how to translate business problems into data problems and have the technical acumen required to get the data into the right shape for production so data scientists can focus on leveraging it with hard-core modeling techniques. They understand aspects of programming but are not programming experts or wizards.

From a salary perspective, this data translator sits

between the data analyst, who's inexpensive, and the data scientist, who's very expensive. This role creates a better alignment between an organization's costs and ROI. The data translator helps solve one of the biggest gaps in the machine-intelligence revolution: bridging the self-defeating gap between technical and non-technical teams by creating a seamless and effective communication process. From my experience, any large organization looking to transform itself into a data-driven enterprise needs to employ them as a critical part of its change-management process.

PART III

CASE STUDIES: DEVELOPING CRITICAL THINKING ABOUT DATA AND MODELING

The first part of this book provided you with an education and the tools for developing data literacy and a machine-intelligence mindset. The second part went step-by-step through the data-science workflow. With cutting-edge industry scenarios, the case studies in the third part will reinforce the learning objectives of the first two parts, teaching you how to think about each phase and step in the data science workflow and how to critique the output of learning models. This will of course involve some repetition of the general principles set forth in Parts 1 and 2 in the context of each case study.

The case studies are meant to have a general application. They involve both modeling and evaluation techniques that can be applied to any industry, not just the industry examined in the specific case study. These are intended to help you, as an executive, to develop critical thinking about leveraging data with modeling techniques that can be applied to your enterprise and push your business forward.

After reading through these case studies, my hope is that you will be able to go back to your daily routine and start thinking about how to translate your top business problems into data and modeling solutions. By creating use cases, you will be able to start transforming your organization and ensuring it survives in the Fourth Industrial Revolution.

CHAPTER 11

CASE STUDY 1

BANKING/FINANCE

THE ASK STEPS
Ask

**Asking great quesions
that can be answered
with data**

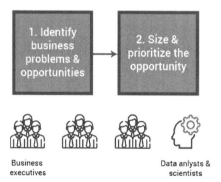

Business
executives

Data anlysts &
scientists

In this hypothetical case study, we'll dive into a well-known data-science application in the financial industry. Any number of high-performing, efficient data-analysis models can transform this vertical by redefining loan structures to better identify creditworthy customers and enhance revenue.

This case study focuses on the creation of a machine-learning application able to redefine who creditworthy customers are. Traditional banking looks at descriptive outcomes, for example, your credit score, years of employment, family status, household income, and similar measures. Typically, banks evaluate creditworthy clients by examining these direct measures, but this is not a smart or efficient way to identify creditworthy customers in an era of wealth of data.

For example, if you, as a customer, have a significant amount of money in the bank and are employed, your credit score should be just fine. Intuitively, your bank should give you a loan or credit card because you have a healthy bank account. However, let's say you didn't work in the last three months. Your credit score might be damaged. If you were to ask for a loan, the bank would look at that metric and, even though you have money in your account, your credit score would probably indicate that you're not a creditworthy client. This old-fashioned method of identifying creditworthy customers is clearly inefficient, leaving millions of dollars in interest and other fees on the table.

Machine-intelligence applications are disrupting this approach by discerning new patterns in the data that identify the likelihood of a customer defaulting. The new patterns decide whether the bank should offer additional products like loans or credit cards based on both historical and dynamic data.

This study examines a hypothetical, specific case in the financial industry. Customers were being denied lines of credit because of existing, outdated credit policies based entirely on data from credit bureaus and by following the bank's internal policy and guidelines. However, the reasons for declining the applications didn't necessarily indicate that a consumer's credit was bad.

To take another example, if you've been self-employed for only a short time, with your potential average income unknown and unsubstantiated, your credit rating might be damaged. But if you have money, have worked all your life, and suddenly decide to take a break or become self-employed, this shouldn't damage your credit score if your payment history is clean.

However, the data shows that the current method rejects 41 percent of credit lines and 39 percent of loan applications. The bank's head of unsecured products would like to better identify creditworthy customers and drive the credit-card and unsecured loan business forward. She wants to adopt a different system and create a different policy structure that better identifies creditworthy customers in order to grow business.

Knowing that 40 percent of all unsecured product applications are rejected, we also know the current system isn't smart enough. Forty percent is a large number and indicates a big opportunity. So, as an executive, you've now gone through the **first step** in the ask process: identifying a top business problem that needs to be solved.

How can the bank approve more unsecured loan applications by waiving certain non-regulatory criteria that result in low-risk customers being rejected? Using advanced modeling techniques on a rich data set, you want to see if you can both respect the regulatory constraints imposed by government and industry agencies, while also waiving certain non-regulatory internal policies to identify creditworthy customers among those currently rejected. The bank will then approve more unsecured loans and credit cards, leverage its transaction base, and generate more revenue.

The **second step** in the ask phase is to do a back-of-the-envelope calculation of the opportunity. Always estimate potential ROI before embarking on a machine-intelligence project to make sure it's feasible and has a high-impact potential. It's time to do a quick sanity check and figure out if the opportunity is worthwhile.

In this case, as an executive at the bank, you know that a five-to-ten percent reduction in application rejections has the potential to increase revenue by $1 to $2 million in the first year, and even more in the second and third years. Doing a back-of-the-envelope approach, you look at what would happen if the 40 percent rejection rate were lowered to 35 percent or even 30 percent. The potential uplift in revenue from granting unsecured loans or credit cards to 5 percent or 10 percent of customers now being rejected is $1 to $2 million dollars in this case.

This simple back-of-the-envelope approach makes you realize you have gold on the table. This project is a worthy one with a potentially high positive impact and should be investigated further.

Acquire

Acquiring & preparing data for analysis

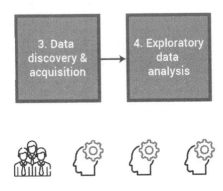

The **third step** in the overall process is data discovery: figuring out what type of data is relevant to the analysis and needs to be collected. For instance, customer demographics will clearly be important. What type of product or products does this customer already have? How many of each? What's the transaction data for each product? This will tell you how much money the customers have, how many transactions they make, and the interest rates they are charged.

Communication channels are another important data feed. What's the best way to communicate with specific customers and customer types? How should you send them messages? What types of messages should you send? What messages resonate?

You can also enhance the internal data set by exploring external data sets, which might reveal additional customer preferences and characteristics. Think both about the data you can leverage internally and how you can enhance this by sourcing external data.

The **fourth step** is Exploratory Data Analysis (EDA), in which you become more familiar with the data, learning what it reveals before embarking on the modeling phase. The EDA phase can answer questions about whether you have the right data to answer the initial business problem. Is the data in the right shape? Is it labeled? Is there enough data, or do we need more? Do we need to refine the original business question with respect to the story the data tells us and the findings we get when we process the data we have?

As the expression goes, to get to know Rome, you have to walk down the city's streets and alleys. The EDA similarly helps you familiarize yourself with the data in order to identify interesting features. For example, are there any specific trends in the data that need to be controlled for? Are there any outliers that could skew the analysis? If so, perhaps they should be removed or balanced in some other way. EDA is the point in the data-science workflow where you do an in-depth investigation and get to know the data better.

In doing this analysis, the bank's technical team identified more than 2,000 different features and variables. This may not be such great news. Such a large number of variables might cause your models to overfit to specific data, and when an overfitted model is fed new data, it will trigger incorrect results.

So the team looked at the initial set of 2,000 variables and identified the ones with the highest likelihood of finding the right answers to our initial business questions: Is this customer creditworthy or not? Will this customer default on a credit card or unsecured loan? Looking more closely is critical at this point, and by doing so, the technical team was able to reduce the 2,000 features and variables to a small subset of forty-four. These forty-four features were identified as the most important in answering the initial business question of identifying whether a customer would default. This is a critical step in the acquire phase, as it will enable the data to be put in the right format for processing.

In this case, the bank did an EDA on the following types of data, among others:

- Time elapsed between billing and payment

- The rate at which unsecured-loan customers default
- The rate, if any, at which such defaults are recovered

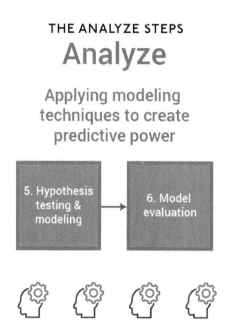

THE ANALYZE STEPS

Analyze

Applying modeling techniques to create predictive power

Now your technical team at the bank has learned about your data, normalized it, removed outliers, and controlled for seasonality and similar trends. It's now production time, when the data is input into the machine-intelligence model. This is the **fifth step** in the overall process, and the first in the analyze phase.

In this case, the financial institution decided to run three different models since it's important to run multiple models to find the best fit: there is no single winning horse in the game! The models chosen were those mentioned in Chapter 8:

- Logistic regression
- Neural network
- Random forest

These three different models were run, and in the **sixth** step, their results were benchmarked and evaluated. It is critical for executives and business leaders to familiarize themselves with this step because this is where you determine the usability of the output from the model's data analysis and processing. This output may be numeric or graphic, but whatever the case, you as an executive need to know how to criticize and evaluate machine-intelligence models based on output—what the model predicts—so that your decisions are smart and unbiased.

So the crucial question is, how do you evaluate the performance of any of these models? Some executives say they can evaluate machine-intelligence models by comparing them to already-existing methods and models. In attempting to identify whether a customer is creditworthy, they compare the results of the machine-intelligence model to the results from the existing system, seeing if the new models trigger predictions that make sense and resonate intuitively.

You can also examine how much error a model generates. We live in a world of uncertainty. Models try to find best-fit patterns, but they won't be 100 percent accurate. There will be some margin of error between the observed data and the model's predictive power, which yields uncertain results.

To clarify, observed data is certain, as it has already been determined before being collected. Predictions are best approximations. If there is a large margin of error between observed data and predictions, the model will have generated biased results.

Both the model's predictive power and margin of error must be carefully examined. How meaningful are its predictions? How significant are the features we input into the model? We can look at the true positives and true negatives the model generates to determine how well the model behaves with respect to the data that has been input.

Some common and popular model-evaluation techniques, also mentioned in Chapter 8, are:

- Cross-validation
- Confusion metric
- Accuracy, precision, and recall

The confusion metric is a table that shows the number

of predictions for each class compared to the number of instances that actually belong to that class. It helps you obtain a general overview of the types of mistakes a particular machine-intelligence algorithm makes. The confusion metric can show us the model's accuracy, its true positives, its false positives, and its measures of sensitivity and specificity.

		Predicted Class	
		No	Yes
Observed Class	No	TN	FP
	Yes	FN	TP

TN	True Negative
FP	False Positive
FN	False Negative
TP	True Positive

To contextualize this in terms of the case study's original business problem, the observed data in this case will be whether a customer has defaulted or not. The accuracy of the model's predictive power hinges on whether a customer will be able to pay back a loan or use a credit card properly.

As previously mentioned, precision and recall are better measures of predictive power than accuracy, but there are some trade-offs and pitfalls to pay attention to in both cases. When considering how precise our predictions are in comparison to the training or observed data set, higher precision means the model will miss some cases.

Take panning for gold, for example. Imagine yourself standing in a California river during the Gold Rush. There's a pan in your hand as you try to scoop gold out of the river.

With precision uppermost in your mind, you scoop just once and look at the pan to see how many gold nuggets, as opposed to other stones the pan now contains. Think of a model's precision in a similar manner. The model scoops nuggets out of the data. Precision is how well your scooping technique is able to collect and find gold from among all the other stones in the river. With high precision, you are successfully able to identify the gold among all other stones collected.

If the river is known to have gold in it and you gather and look at only a few stones, it means you have higher probability of finding gold in the few stones you pick up in a single scoop. In statistics, this is called sample-size bias. However, when you only scoop out a few stones, you leave the rest and therefore miss several opportunities to find gold.

Looking at this in terms of a creditworthy unsecured loan applications, you could narrow your sample size and just look at the applications that exhibit the highest precision. The model could generate customers with the highest credit scores or the lowest default rates, but the total number would be incredibly small. You'd miss out on customers with lower precision rates but who are still worthy applicants.

Recall has a different set of trade-offs. It involves determining how good a model is at identifying all events. If precision is about scooping out a single pan of gold to identify the smallest percentage of customers with the highest precision, recall is the opposite. It tries to gather all possible cases by looking at the entire data set—all 40 percent of rejected customers—and figure out how many positive events the model correctly identifies. It pans the river for gold not once but as often as possible.

If you're an executive in the bank's risk department, you would be interested in looking at the problem horizontally and identifying all cases. The risk department wants to measure and manage the bank's overall risk. It doesn't want to only measure premium-customer risk, as the precision model did, because such a model neglects all other relevant cases.

To manage overall risk, the risk department wants to go as wide and encompass as many cases as possible. When panning the river, a risk executive would want to scoop up as many stones as possible and identify how many are gold. What are the true positives?

Recall is about casting as wide a net as possible. You try to determine how many gold nuggets your model was able to catch, no matter how precise it was. Some stones will be gold, some won't. What matters is gathering most of the stones in the river.

Ultimately, you must look at both measures, precision and recall, and find the right balance between them. Different people in your business will be interested in different evaluation metrics and techniques. Recall will resonate more with overall risk managers, and precision more with underwriters. Trade off between them and be careful how you interpret each.

Other model evaluation techniques with names such as the Receiver Operating Characteristic Curve (ROC Curve), Gini Coefficient, and Root Mean Squared Error (RMSE) were also mentioned in Chapter 8. The idea here is that you don't need to become an expert in how these model evaluation techniques work from a mathematical or statistical perspective. You just need a general understanding of what they mean and how to interpret them from macro-level perspectives: magnitude, positive/negative, trade-offs, etc. What's the bottom line?

Among all the evaluation metric techniques, you will focus on the few that make sense both from a data and business perspective. In this case, you and your technical team chose to use two of these metrics to benchmark the models, say RMSE and the Gini Coefficient.

In this case, the bank wants a *low* RMSE and a **high** Gini Coefficient. These are our "winning horses," which, taken together, will effectively enable you to evaluate your model's predictive power.

THE ACT STEPS
Act

Interpreting the outcomes
& operationalizing
across the enterprise

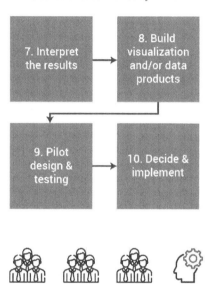

The **seventh step** in the data-science workflow, the first step in the act phase, is to start interpreting the model's results. Are they aligned with your intuition, and how can you act, based upon what you now know, to solve the initial business problem?

You should always compare a machine-intelligence model's results with those generated by the previous method. You're now able to identify additional good customers that the previous system marked as bad. The model now captures 87 percent of all creditworthy applicants, a significantly higher percentage than before.

In this case, the model identified an additional 12 percent of "good customers" by looking at the entire customer database and identifying the customers with low default rates and statistically high creditworthiness. This will revolutionize the financial institution's business, as there are now 12 percent more customers it can offer financial products to, with corresponding increases in revenue, while maintaining the same risk level for the business.

Let's look at some interesting predictors and see what can we learn from them. One of the most significant predictors used as input into the machine-intelligence model is the *monthly average of balance inquiries*. The more customers check their balance in a three-month period, the less likely they are to be creditworthy.

If you're short on money, what would you do? Would you check your balance frequently or not? Obviously, it's more likely you'd check it frequently. The model suggests that if you do this—a factor not taken into account in the previous system—you're a risky customer with a higher potential default rate, and this squares with our intuition.

A second interesting predictor is customers' *average number of monthly transactions* or deposits over a six-month period. Lower transaction rates imply lower default rates.

Another predictor is the *number of products* a customer already has with the bank. The more products, the more often the customer has already been through some sort of credit-score investigation. Yet another predictor is number *of months of employment.* The longer you've been employed, the less likely you will default. All this resonates intuitively.

One of the best ways of interpreting outcomes is through the **eighth step** in the workflow, building visualizations that will demonstrate the model's predictions so that everyone in the organization can understand them and make quick decisions. A great, as opposed to good, data scientist is one who knows how to communicate the model's results artistically.

If a member of the technical team is not able to communicate data and predictions in an artistic, visual way so that everyone can understand them, they've essentially failed. Data visualization—interpreting results to make sure they resonate intuitively and correspond with previous experience and knowledge—is a crucial step in the data-science workflow.

The **ninth step** is to demonstrate the ROI realized

through the new machine-intelligence model. The goal of the machine-intelligence model was, after having taken all the regulatory aspects as constraints, to waive as many non-regulatory and internal policies as feasible by looking at new trends in the data. More specifically, the goal was to transfer as many customers who are creditworthy from the "bad-customer" to the "good-customer" group, expecting that the default rate will decrease.

Let's say the financial institution increases credit approvals by 7 to 8 percent. This is within the 12 percent range the model generated but a bit more conservative and cautious.

Your earlier back-of-the envelope calculations predicted that a 5 to 10 percent reduction in rejection rates would generate $1 to $2 million in additional revenue in the first year. Actually, however, there is a 12 percent reduction in rejection rates, so the ROI will be even higher.

Machine-intelligence technology and techniques help you both discover new trends and patterns from historical data about your customer base and, while respecting regulatory constraints, find a larger pool of customers who are identified as creditworthy, while maintaining the overall risk for the bank at the same level. This method discovers ways to detect creditworthy clients based on actual historical transaction data, as opposed to the previous system, based on internal policies, which generated a 40 percent rejection rate by ignoring nuances and looking only at large-scale patterns and trends.

The **tenth step** is change management: making decisions and implementing them. Again, models by themselves will not add value. Implementing and operationalizing them requires a cultural change: people in the organization must become more open to the model's predictions and be able to access them. Start transforming your organization into a data-driven enterprise that cultivates a culture of looking at and leveraging data to make decisions. Continue by transforming your organization into a model-driven enterprise that can respond to your model's predictions quickly and effectively.

Model-driven enterprises can react quickly to their models' predictions. If an organization cannot best respond quickly to the predictions a model generates, it will not be able to realize $2 million in additional revenue the first year.

Change management is crucial. Make, fulfill, and track the offers the model recommends that you decide among, and you will improve the model over time. Consider if you need to enhance your systems: most of the time, you will need to figure out how to embed a new modeling technique into your current process. In this case study, the bank needs to operationalize the new model in its current systems so that loan and credit officers can make quick, automatic decisions about whether to make an offer to a customer or not.

As previously mentioned, 60 percent of machine-intelligence projects are not implemented or abandoned because executives and management teams do not think about how to operationalize models at the beginning of the journey. But executives should be expected to think about such issues. Always consider the operational and cultural changes that will need to be made so that when you come to the tenth step, you can quickly realize an uplift in revenue.

SHORT-TERM AND LONG-TERM STRATEGIES

It's true that, in most cases, a system enhancement will be required, and this will probably require engineering time. Such enhancement won't happen in a day—which is why you need to start thinking about it very early in the process—but that doesn't mean you should abandon the project or delay acting on the model's predictions as soon as they have been tested and validated.

Many organizations make this mistake. Executives think, "Oh, we need a year and a half for system enhancement. It takes a lot of time." They ignore the model's predictions until they can be operationalized within the system. This is the wrong approach because the model needs to be trained: the iterative process of inputting results will improve the model over time.

A short-term strategy is crucial if you want to realize ROI. In this case, the short-term strategy would involve manually reviewing a "white list" of customers and checking it against all applications. If the applicant is on the model-generated white list, make an offer and see if it is converted. Each time it is, you will realize ROI.

In the long term, you should go through a full system enhancement that will generate automatic notifications and recommendations for matching creditworthy customers with products. If you invest in integrating new credit-score modeling into your decision process so customers will automatically be notified of new offers and financial products, revenue growth will be driven further upward.

CHAPTER 12

CASE STUDY 2

E-COMMERCE AND MARKETING FROM RETENTION AND ENGAGEMENT TO UPSELLING

THE ASK STEPS
Ask

Asking great quesions that can be answered with data

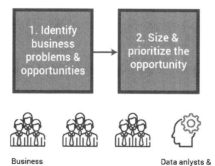

A financial institution developed a digital product that demonstrated strong initial adoption in a regional market. However, conversions then stagnated. After initial enthusiasm, customers stopped interacting or interacted far less frequently with the product. The data shows there's been a 50 percent drop-off in total transactions in the past few months, and 40 percent of current customers are no longer engaged.

The management team discussed the problem and decided to launch a viral marking campaign to drive product growth. Take a few seconds to think about what you'd do if the others on your management team decided that a marketing campaign would solve the problem at hand. Is this the right solution?

This case study shows that executives often adopt a traditional or typical solutions to common problems. This may or may not be the best solution to the initial business problem in the short, medium, or long term. What wasn't done was to validate assumptions by looking at and analyzing the data. Such a data-driven decision might well have led to a new or different approach. Only by investigating the data can you be sure you're not headed in the wrong direction.

In fact, the marketing campaign did not solve the engagement and conversion-rate problem. As business leader, you need to have the courage to say, "Hey, I've thought about it, and I don't think that a marketing campaign is the right solution. We need to consider a different direction." Of course, if you're going to make such a statement, you need to have the data to back it up.

The business problem is to improve overall engagement and retention rates. Can you leverage the data you have to develop strategies that will drive product growth? This is **step 1** in the ask phase of the data-science workflow.

You then need to start translating your business problems into data problems. Think about what the data opportunities are. Ask great questions that will help solve the problem by leveraging the data you already possess.

One such question is whether you can leverage product-related data to identify why customers are churning or disengaged. This would involve an analysis of engaged and disengaged customers that compares these two groups' behaviors when interacting with the product. Other questions that might spark the answer to this problem are: When in the process do customers become disengaged? Is it in the beginning, middle, or end of the customer's online journey? In the transaction phase? Or is it in later steps that customers log off, disappear, and don't come back?

Here's a hint: unseen technical problems are causing customer impatience and disengagement. This is something the financial institution didn't see right away because the management team decided to launch a viral marketing campaign before doing a thorough data analysis.

Step 2 in the ask phase is to size the opportunity. What is this project's potential ROI? Do a back-of-the-envelope calculation to get some ballpark numbers. You only want to deal with projects that will have high visibility and a high impact on the business.

If there's a 5–10 percent increase in customer engagement for this specific product in the targeted regional market, there will be potential uplift in total assets under management of about $1 billion in the first year. This was calculated by multiplying the average amount of customers' annual transactions by 5–10 percent of the customer base.

One billion dollars: gold had definitely been left on the table. This is a big opportunity for the financial institution.

Acquire

Acquiring & preparing data for analysis

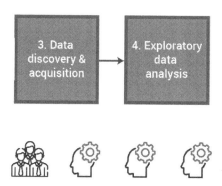

In the acquire phase, you start with **step 3** of the overall workflow, which is figuring out what data you have, so you can begin leveraging it to spark the solutions to the problem. What type of data would be relevant to collect for this analysis?

Such data might include customer demographics, product holdings, transaction data, risk and credit history, CRMs, and dispatch-center data. Click-stream data is particularly important and encompasses all relevant data obtained from the app and website: amount of time spent on the site, when and how many times customers click on a link, the number of times customers log into the system, how long they stay before logging off, whether there were technical issues or errors, and so on.

General-behavior data refers to how customers interact with a product or marketing campaign: whether, for example, after being sent a marketing message, they went to the store to redeem the offer, whether they accessed additional marketing material online or via email, and so on. Taken all together, this data gives a 360-degree view of customers' engagement and interaction with the financial institution and its products and offerings.

Aside from internal data, you can explore opportunities to obtain external data, for example, from the Google Play Store. Google Analytics could also provide additional behavioral data.

Step 2 in the acquire phase, **step 4** overall, is to go through an Exploratory Data Analysis (EDA), which involves getting the data into the right shape so it can be input into and processed by your machine-intelligence models. The data needs to be made ready for production.

EDA is critical because, before you go through modeling techniques, you need to get to know your data inside out. Is the data in the right shape? Is it properly labeled? Is there enough of it? This phase can also help you figure out if there are any trends and outliers that could skew the analysis and need to be dealt with.

The following graph is a churn analysis for four different regional markets over time.

Churn % by Quarter

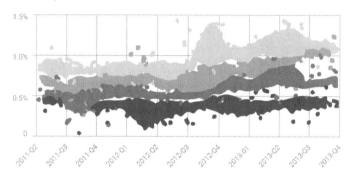

It shows churn by percentage per quarter in the four different regions where the product was launched. The top, orange segment represents the regional market where there is a high churn rate and which is the focus of the analysis. You see an upward trend, and over time, a lot of disengaged customers. In April 2012, for example, there was a worrying peak in churn rate. A lot of customers left around this time, so maybe there was a problem related to this specific month that caused customers to churn. It's something that needs to be investigated.

Now look at this related table:

CUSTOMER	AREA	LOG IN ATTEMPTS	LOG IN SECONDS	TIME SPENT C-SERV	PRODUCT	PROMOTION	HOLIDAY	TRANSACTION VALUE	MAX TIME SPENT	MIN TIME SPENT	TRANSACTIONS	ACTIVE CHURN?
0	KS	30	128	475	382-4657	NO	YES	11.01	128.0	2.70	1245	0
1	OH	3	17	15	371-7191	NO	YES	11.45	13.7	3.70	123	0
2	NJ	52	137	45	358-1921	NO	NO	7.32	12.2	3.29	34	1
3	OH	17	84	48	375-9999	YES	NO	8.86	6.6	1.78	34	0
4	OK	31	75	45	330-6626	YES	NO	8.41	10.1	2.79	36	1
5	AL	6	18	5	397-8027	YES	NO	9.18	6.3	1.70	9	0

It shows a number of features of the customer base: where they're located, how many log-in attempts they made, how much time it took them to log in, how much time they spent in the portal, what products they interacted with, whether they had been provided with a promotion in the past sixty days, whether this was during a holiday season, how many transactions they made in a year, and for what total amount. The most important feature to be examined here is: are the customers active or did they churn?

"Active churn" is a binary factor describing whether a customer is still engaged or not. If customers are engaged, they're given a zero value, and if they're not engaged and have churned, they're give a value of one. Looking, for instance, at the two customers whose data is tracked in lines 2 and 4 of the chart, you'll see they are no longer active.

Now, the question is whether this data can be leveraged to answer the initial business problem and solve the problem of engagement and retention.

Take a minute to think about some important questions: What is your organization's current process for seizing such worthy opportunities? Who do you go to in order to move forward? What is the mindset? How will you get funding?

From a data prioritization perspective, this project has high visibility and a potentially high impact on the organization in terms of ROI. There is gold on the table. How do you get it?

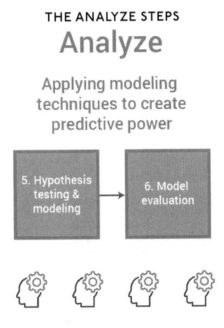

THE ANALYZE STEPS

Analyze

Applying modeling techniques to create predictive power

The first step in the analyze phase—**step 5** overall—is to start thinking about which machine-intelligence models you want to employ in your analysis. You and your technical team will analyze the engagement problem by doing churn modeling that attempts to figure out the differences between engaged, active customers and customers who have churned or disengaged. Machine-intelligence techniques will be employed to find the different patterns within the data associated with these two customer groups. Which data features contribute to customer churn?

As always, multiple models will be run to find the best fit, as there's never a single winning horse at this phase. Two of the three models here are the same as those employed in the first case study: neural networks and random forest. The other model is one known as k-nearest neighbors.

K-NEAREST NEIGHBORS

The k-nearest neighbors model is a classification method. Here, k refers to the number of classes we want to sort the data into, and the technique involves pattern recognition. So k could equal 3, 10, or any other integer, which will represent the number of classes the data is divided into. The algorithm is designed to come up with an optimum figure for k, the one that yields the number of classes that will best separate the data into the classes most appropriate for your business problem. Then you can target each one directly and offer a specify remedy, solution, or offer.

As described in Chapter 8, a "deep learning" neural network is a model that imitates the non-linear flow of data in our brains. This model is both very sophisticated and computationally expensive. "Random forest" is a decision-tree model.

Running the three different models yields three outputs. **Step 6** in the overall workflow—step 2 in the analyze phase—is to find the best fit. You and your technical team's job is to benchmark the various outputs and evaluate the models.

A confusion matrix, which shows us true positives and false positives in the predictive class, based on what is known about the observed data class, is then used to evaluate the results of all of these models. The following confusion-matrix graphic shows that each model has different precision and recall levels:

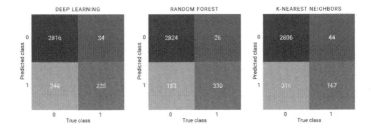

Precision is the ratio of correctly predicted positive values to the total number of predicted positive values, whether correct or not. The *k*-nearest neighbor has an accuracy level of 80 percent, the neural network 87 percent, and the random forest 93 percent. Looking at precision levels, the winning model, the one we should adopt, is random forest.

A leadership question here is: How would *you* evaluate

the performance of these models? Is precision the right metric here?

While precision has pitfalls and needs to be used with caution, it can be a good heuristic or rule-of-thumb technique. That is the case here. Again, a simpler model—random forest—is shown to outperform a more sophisticated neural network or deep-learning model.

The confusion matrix also compares recall, another important evaluative technique, for each model. Recall is the ratio of correctly predicted positive values to actual positive values. Here, it tells us how often the model correctly predicts when an individual customer will churn. By this measure, random forest again outperforms the two competing techniques: it has a recall rate of 68 percent, as opposed to the neural network's 50 percent and k-nearest neighbors' 35 percent.

By doing such benchmarking and comparison, we've now been able to identify the winning horse. By both measures, precision and recall, random forest is the model we should use in addressing this business problem.

Act

Interpreting theoutcomes
& operationalizing
across the enterprise

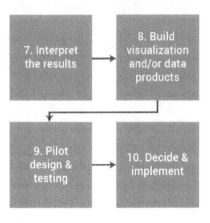

The first step in the act phase, **step 7** in the overall workflow, focuses on interpreting the results your machine-intelligence model yields and figuring out if those results align with your intuition. The model's churn analysis should help you: (1) understand which potentially active customers are not engaged; and (2) identify this problem's probable cause.

There are a number of interesting features from the analysis that can help us understand why customers churn.

The first non-traditional predictor is *log-in attempts*. The more log-in attempts per session customers make, the more likely it is that they'll churn. Pay attention to this. If a significant number of customers try to log-in five times per session, a technical issue may be involved. If you know that, you can take action to change it.

The second notable feature is the *average response time* between screens in both the website and app versions of the product. The more time it takes for the system to respond to a click and upload a new screen, the higher the churn rate. People churn because they get impatient.

Another factor is whether a customer has received a *promotion* in the past 30 days or not. If the financial institution doesn't reach out to their customers with promotions in any thirty-day period, the analysis shows those customers are likely to churn. The final notable feature is number of products. The more products customers have, the less likely they will churn because they're more highly engaged with the financial institution as a whole.

Churn analysis will not only help you determine the probability that a customer will churn—our y target—but will also explain, by analyzing different features and patterns distinguishing churners from active customers, why they churn.

Now we can identify and focus on solving some of the

underlying problems causing churn. This will involve both fixing technical problems and figuring out how to better engage with customers. More frequent and regular promotions tailored to specific groups, even small ones, might be a great way to incentivize increased engagement. As you move forward, always make sure the results make sense and resonate with your intuition.

The best way to figure out which customers to engage with is through data visualization: **step 8** in the data-science workflow. Let's look at the quantitative rather than qualitative results from this churn model: the probability a customer will churn. Think in terms of probabilities because these will form the basis of important executive decisions.

The following table visualizes the of the machine-learning models' predictions, with customer segments arranged in percentiles based on that their total assets under management and the probability that customers in that segment will churn—our y target.

GROUP	PRED PROB	COUNT	TRUE PROB	AUM SS
0	0.0	1765345	0.028329	971671
1	0.1	693678	0.025974	974026
2	0.2	269678	0.070632	929368
3	0.3	123368	0.138211	861789
4	0.4	77798	0.350649	649351
5	0.5	545469	0.518519	581481
6	0.6	73567	0.835616	494384
7	0.7	76769	0.855263	384737
8	0.8	70865	0.957143	272857
9	0.9	75145	0.973333	196667
10	1.0	58568	1.000000	128743

Count — pred_prob

The probability that customers in the first four segments—segments 0, 1, 2, and 3—will churn is relatively low: 0–50 percent. These customers are unlikely to churn and represent a very low opportunity in terms of revenue uplift. They are not the problem and do not represent a major risk.

Moving to segments 4, 5, and 6, the probability of customer churn is higher: 40–60 percent. The risk that customers in these tiers will churn is in the medium range. When we go to the seventh, eighth, ninth, and tenth segments, we see that the probability of churning spikes. These customers present a high risk.

As an executive, you need to make a data-driven decision on which groups to target. Looking at both risk and assets-under-management figures for these segments, it becomes obvious that customer segments 7 through 10 should be targeted. While there are fewer customers in these segments, their assets-under-management numbers are high, and a lot of money can be saved if you prevent them from churning.

From a cost and operations perspective, it doesn't make sense to target the first group—segments 0 through 3—which have a low probability of churning. Targeting the second and third groups—segments 4 through 7 and 8 through 10—might yield better results with respect to the allocation of effort and resources.

All executives and organizations live in a world of constraints. If your organization had all the money and talent in the world, you would probably start targeting all segments beginning with segment 4 and up. However, it would be expensive to dedicate a lot of resources and capital to customers whose churn probability is 40 percent. An executive decision must be made on which groups make the most sense to target based on budgetary and other constraints. Even targeting just one segment will take a lot of work.

It would also be costly to implement a decision to introduce additional promotions and new incentives to a large number of customers. There would, however, be a significant difference in the resources required to target segments 8 and up as opposed to segments 4 and up. It would be far less expensive to direct promotions only to segments 8, 9, and 10, which have fewer customers who are more likely to churn. As an executive, you must decide where the cutoff point will be. In all probability, it will be segments 8 and above.

Step 9 in the overall machine-intelligence workflow is to demonstrate ROI from a pilot initiative. The original projection was that a 5 to 10 percent increase in customer engagement would potentially yield $1 billion in additional assets under management in the first year. This figure can now be calculated more accurately. Look at what the ROI would be if the churn rate in groups 8 through 10 was reduced significantly. Is there an actual revenue uplift of $1 billion in the first year? In step 9, you need to revalidate the initial ROI projection, after piloting and testing, and make sure it is aligned with your goal before operationalizing and implementing your machine-intelligence model throughout the organization.

Step 10 is to make and implement operational decisions. It's important to think in terms of both a short-term minimum viable product (MVP) and a long-term strategy. You must devise a strategy to implement and leverage the results from the model in the short term prior to making an investment in system enhancement. Don't let the costs of the latter prevent you from operationalizing the project immediately and making short-term gains.

What would your short-term and long-term implementation and operationalization strategies be?

Here are some ideas. In the **short term**, you can start looking at the features that cause customers to churn, such as the technical problems, demonstrated by the data on log-in attempts and app-response time, mentioned earlier, and act to correct them. Fix these and set different thresholds for triggering notifications of such problems to relevant IT and product personnel. Automatic thresholds will flag issues immediately so that they can be resolved quickly before customers begin to get annoyed and start churning. Other features related to the online customer/ user experience should be also investigated.

Perhaps you should also manually track customers with the highest probability of churn and reach out to them, either individually by phone or through specific marketing campaigns or offers relevant to their churn risk. You may want to have your marketing department reach out to segment 10, segments 9 and 10, or segments 8, 9, and 10 with promotions at least once every thirty days. You've now expanded your intuition, knowledge, and ability to act by leveraging large amounts of data through machine-intelligence models.

The **long-term solution** might be to build a system that will automatically generate contextual marketing campaigns. Perhaps you will start by targeting segments 8 and 9. Figure out what types of marketing campaigns and messaging will highly resonate with these specific customer groups and have the system automatically generate promotions that will keep them engaged. This can occur when your organization has reached a level of maturity that has shifted it from a data-driven to a model-driven enterprise: one that responds quickly to predictions from machine-learning model predictions and automatically generates content-marketing campaigns to ensure your business is growing and expending its market share.

LET'S SELL MORE: BECOMING PROACTIVE
RATHER THAN MERELY REACTIVE

Let's return to the original business problem. You and your organization have an issue with disengaged customers and want to figure out how to drive product growth. Churn analysis will help you solve only half of this initial business problem: engagement and retention. How do you drive product growth? Now that we have solved the churn issue and have an active, engaged group of customers, how can we start upselling to drive product growth and additional revenue?

As mentioned several times before, the process you are engaged in is iterative. Having gone through the ten steps of the machine-intelligence workflow to deal reactively with customer disengagement, you can now iterate though the workflow once again to deal proactively with growth and upselling.

THE ASK PHASE: SECOND ITERATION

So let's assume the engagement problem has been solved. Whereas at the beginning of the process only 40 percent or 50 percent of your customers were engaged, now 90 percent are. Now the question is how you can proactively cross-sell, upsell, and drive product growth, as shown in the following illustration:

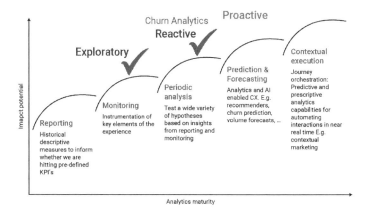

In this second iteration, you are moving up the analytics maturity curve. Now that you know how to retain your customers, how can you make them better offers that are more likely to generate interest and conversion?

We have already gone through the step 1 in the workflow: identify the problem. How do you grow your product?

Then translate the business problem into a data problem. Identify five to seven questions that might spark a solution. For example, can you leverage product-related data to identify which product recommendations to make?

This involves marketing products better: targeting the right messages to the right audiences. If you market intelligently, your messages and offers will resonate strongly with customers, increasing the likelihood of purchase, which in turn will drive growth.

Next, in step 2 of the process, make a back-of-the-envelope ROI calculation. In this case, the answer is obvious: improving offerings and better marketing those products is almost certain to create a significant uplift in revenue. You can extrapolate a number here based on the data provided in the previous analysis.

THE ACQUIRE AND ANALYZE
PHASES: SECOND ITERATION

Now we move to the acquire phase, gathering and preparing your data for production. In the previous iteration, you "acquired" the data then available. The processes put in place then allow you to acquire data generated after the initiative was launched. Most of it is already in place for the second iteration.

You will acquire and process this data with a number of recommendation-engine techniques. Product recommendation engines typically collect, sort, and analyze data. The analysis finds patterns in the data that generate recommendations. The following diagram shows the architecture of a product-recommendation system:

We want to let the machine learn patterns in the data to make product recommendations to customers in a dynamic fashion

The architecture of the system can be represented by the following diagram:

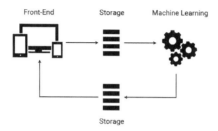

The front end is the interface customers interact with. Data from these interactions is collected and stored. Machine-intelligence techniques are then employed to generate results, iteratively triggering customer decisions and actions at the interface. Whether a customer converts an offer or not is recorded as another data point and stored. An OODA loop has been created and continues to iterate.

During this second iteration, the analyze phase is closely linked to the acquire phase and is already under way. The principal machine-intelligence techniques used in building recommendation engines and analyzing the data they collect were discussed in Chapter 2. More information about these techniques can be found in Appendix B.

Content-based filtering gives customers recommendations for products or content similar to ones they have already viewed or purchased. **Clustering** recommends content and products to all customers in a specific demographic cluster—such as "premium clients"—no matter what action any individual in the cluster may have taken or not taken. A premium client will receive recommendations for the same services and products that other premium clients get. With **collaborative filtering**, the system provides recommendations based on the similarities in customers' behaviors. If two customers, for instance, live in the same area and have similar expenses, and one decides to apply for a loan, a financial institution will offer the other customer the same or a similar loan as well.

THE ACT PHASE

The last phase of the data-science workflow, **act**, is entered once the recommendation engine goes online. As more data is iteratively gathered over time, recommendations continue to improve. The system optimizes based on the additional input, such as whether an offer has been converted or not, as shown in the following illustration.

A better way to upsell the products

Read by both users

Similar users

Read by her,
recommended to him

**Deliver targeted recommendations
to increase market share**

FEEDBACK LOOP

As you have probably noticed, the workflow can be compressed and move more quickly following the first iteration of a machine-intelligence initiative. As you continue to iterate, you continue to climb the analytics maturity curve shown in the following diagram:

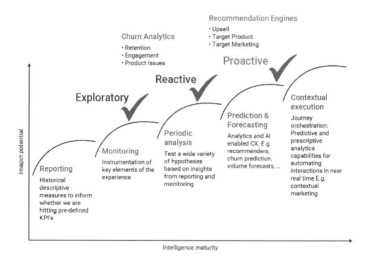

To review quickly, the exploratory and reactive phases involved churn analytics, which helped solve issues of retention and engagement. This was the first iteration of the machine-intelligence initiative covered in this case study.

Then, to drive product growth, prediction and forecasting were employed through the use of a recommendation engine, which helps upsell products to customers who are now fully engaged. This is the initiative's second iteration.

Recommendation engines help determine the right products and messages for the right customers. They enable organizations to become smarter and more proactive, cultivating more opportunities to upsell by leveraging data with modeling techniques and progressing along the analytics-maturity curve to a state of "higher intelligence" and greater automation by looking at historical data and behavioral patterns of customer, client, or user preferences.

CHAPTER 13

CASE STUDY 3

SMART-CITIES TECHNOLOGY

THE ASK STEPS
Ask

Asking great quesions that can be answered with data

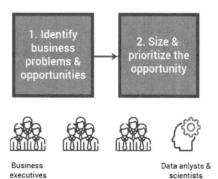

Business executives

Data anlysts & scientists

In this forward-looking case study, **step 1** is, as usual, identifying the business problem. The human population has grown tremendously and is now over the seven billion mark.[18] Fifty percent live in urban areas. This is expected to rise to around 60 percent by 2020. In the developed Western world, that number will be 80 percent.

This massive boost in population brings crowding. Smart-city technology can help alleviate the problems and costs associated with such exponential growth. Traffic congestion due to overpopulation costs the US more than $87.2 billion dollars a year in wasted resources and lost productivity.[19]

What can be done from a modeling perspective with the data cities own to solve this problem? How can the business problem be translated into a solvable data-and-modeling problem?

Advances in machine intelligence now enable software and mobile applications to increasingly incorporate high-

---

18   United Nations, Department of Economic and Social Affairs, Population Division, "World Urbanization Prospects: The 2014 Revision," https://www.compassion.com/multimedia/world-urbanization-prospects.pdf.

19   McKinsey Global Institute, *Smart Cities: Digital Solutions for a More Livable Future*, June 2018, https://www.mckinsey.com/~/media/mckinsey/industries/capital%20projects%20and%20infrastructure/our%20insights/smart%20cities%20digital%20solutions%20for%20a%20more%20livable%20future/mgi-smart-cities-full-report.ashx; Frederico Guerrini, "Traffic Congestion Costs Americans $124 Billion A Year, Report Says," *Forbes*, October 14, 2014, https://www.forbes.com/sites/federicoguerrini/2014/10/14/traffic-congestion-costs-americans-124-billion-a-year-report-says/#7842caabc107.

precision image-recognition capabilities that can sense traffic, traffic jams, parking violations, weather patterns, and road conditions. Models processing this data can then serve as the basis of adaptive signal-control technology, allowing traffic-light timing to change dynamically, based on this real-time data. Such a traffic signal system would be far more efficient than the one we currently have.

Step 2 involves a back-of-the-envelope estimate of the ROI from such a project. The Department of Transportation has determined that this technology could improve travel time by more than 10 percent. The level of improvement could be as high as 50 percent in areas with particularly outdated traffic-light timing. There's clearly an opportunity here to save millions of dollars, run cities more efficiently, and increase the overall utility of roads.

Research estimates a combined market potential of $1.5 trillion globally for smart-city technology with respect not only to transportation but energy, healthcare, and the built environment or infrastructure. A back-of-the-envelope approach suggests that there's a potential market of $1.5 trillion globally for smart-city technology as a whole.

Major US cities, such as Denver, Phoenix, and Pittsburgh, in partnership with large technology companies, are now piloting and testing this technology, especially in high-density areas, such as downtowns and around airports.

Acquire

Acquiring & preparing
data for analysis

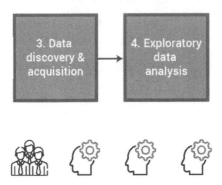

In **step 3**, the first step in the acquire phase, you ask your-self: What type of data would you need to collect and analyze to solve this business problem?

Clearly, you'd need to collect traffic data, like the number and density of cars in specific areas at specific times of day. One important data set is license-plate numbers because you might want to track specific driver behavior over time. You'd also want to collect data on accidents, weather, and floods and other disasters, as well as graphic data, such as how many parking spaces are available in an area at any given time.

Again, the goal here is to create adaptive signal-control

technology to allow traffic lights to change their timing based on real-time dynamic data feeds. The data team assigned to this project identified eighty-eight features to include in the analysis, trimmed back from a much larger set of possible data to avoid overfitting. The team also collected data from third parties, such as parking garages.

Step 4 in the machine-intelligence workflow is exploratory data analysis (EDA), which helps determine if the data we have can answer the business question. Can traffic sensors generate the data needed? Sensors can generate a lot of data, but you want to ensure this data consists of meaningful "signals" rather than just "noise."

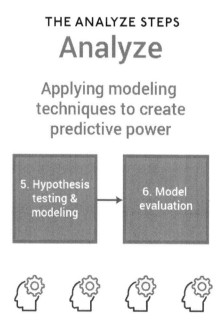

THE ANALYZE STEPS

Analyze

Applying modeling
techniques to create
predictive power

5. Hypothesis testing & modeling → 6. Model evaluation

Step 5—the first step in the analyze phase—is to run multiple machine-intelligence models to find the best fit for creating a dynamic algorithm able to control traffic lights. One such model—the one that ultimately turns out to be the "winning horse" in this case study—is a convolutional neural network. Again, neural networks and their "deep learning" techniques imitate the flow of information in the brain. Without getting into technical details, convolutional neural networks (CNN) specifically imitate the flow of information in the visual cortex and are used in cases, such as the present one, involving visual recognition.

The model's performance is evaluated in **step 6**. How would this be done in this case? One useful evaluative technique is the confusion matrix, which compares the model's predictions for each class of event under consideration with the actual instances of events in each class. Did the model yield the right results? How often did it come up with true positives and true negatives? How many errors and false alarms did the model generate?

The current method of dealing with the problem is manual control, such as having traffic officers control the timing of traffic lights and the flow of traffic on the streets. So the results of the convolutional neural network model should be benchmarked in terms of the performance of the current method—human control—to see whether the machine-intelligence model outperforms the manual, human one.

Many people argue a human can outperform a machine in controlling traffic at a four-way intersection. Traffic officers, they say, are able to optimize flow efficiently. But can our brains always produce optimal outcomes over time? Probably not. Human traffic officers, in the final analysis, are unable to process all the data involving hundreds of cars converging into a single, busy intersection in a city center.

Act

Interpreting theoutcomes
& operationalizing
across the enterprise

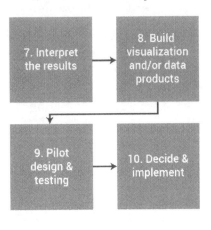

Step 7 in the overall workflow—the first step in the act phase—is to interpret the model's predictions by comparing them with your intuition. Are the results you expected and the actual results in alignment? Data visualization, **step 8**, can further increase your ability to interpret results.

With the images data sensors provide, traffic patterns and driving behaviors can be both seen and forecast. If the sophisticated convolutional neural network machine-intelligence model is properly trained, accuracy rates increase and the number of false or undetected images decreases.

The model also processes data from non-traditional traffic predictors, which generate insights that help us better understand the overall problem. The first such predictor is people driving in circles. The analysis suggests that people driving in circles equates to overcrowded roads or traffic jams. Basically, if you're driving in a circle, you're looking for but can't find a parking spot due to overcrowding or dense traffic.

A second predictor is public transportation. A lot of people using public transportation suggests that an area is overcrowded and there may be traffic congestion. If people know an area is overcrowded, perhaps because there's a football game in the vicinity, they typically use public transportation because they know they won't find parking, or if they do, it will be costly.

A third predictor is carpool lanes. The more people use carpool lanes, the more crowded the roads tend to be; the less people use carpool lanes, the less crowded.

A fourth predictor is the time of day. When it gets late, there is less overcrowding. Weather data is a fifth important predictor because bad weather causes overcrowding and traffic jams. As previously mentioned, lack of parking spots is a great proxy for traffic jams, which is why external data provided by sensors in parking lots can be useful.

Step 9 in the workflow returns to the ROI of the proposed machine-intelligence product or service. Is solving this business problem important enough to warrant the complexity and cost associated with a convolutional neural network?

Google Duplex is an automated system incorporating a convolutional neural network that performs tasks such as booking restaurants and ordering plane tickets. It takes trillions of data points, including voice conversations, to train and curate this model so it will perform accurately in real-time scenarios. Google has been training this model for at least a year, to the point where it interacts well with companies such as United Airlines. Obviously, this is a long, expensive process.

By the same token, however, lessening traffic jams and better understanding overcrowding have the potential to increase transportation efficiency by around 7 to 8 percent. Again, looking at the $82 billion opportunity in the US alone, and the $1.2 trillion opportunity across the globe, it seems like this undertaking has high potential for lessening traffic congestion in cities around the world. This technology could potentially reduce carbon emissions by 62 percent and yield approximately $1.9 million in additional revenue per US city or county.

Step 10 revolves around making and implementing decisions. Could you just implement this system in a city? Probably not immediately, but as you know, models by themselves have no distinct added value. Infrastructure changes will be needed: more cameras and sensors, and traffic lights whose timing can dynamically respond to the machine-intelligence model's predictions. Automated road signs and routing signals must be manufactured and installed.

The model that has been created and tested requires infrastructural change and involves a heavy infrastructural investment. However, as always, it is critical to think about the change management required at the beginning of a machine-intelligence project so that when you arrive at step 10, what will be involved doesn't come as a surprise.

The question then becomes, what can you implement in both the short and long term? What is your strategy?

In the current system, traffic officers control traffic flow manually, based on what they observe in the street. However, they could do so more efficiently based on the model's predictions. Imagine a traffic officer standing in a four-way intersection. If the model predicts the officer should change the light, it will signal that it's time to turn the light green. The traffic officer, receiving this signal on a simple app, will then do so manually. The machine will solve the problem rather than having the traffic officer look around and try to figure out how to respond.

Also, in many cities, especially small ones in the US, traffic lights are controlled from control rooms. This is also true in large international cities, such as Hong Kong and Singapore.

In these cities, you don't find traffic officers in the street. Everything is controlled from control rooms. A short-term "minimal viable product" would involve creating a dashboard for the traffic officers sitting in these control rooms, telling them how and when to change traffic-light settings, which they can do manually.

Of course, the long-term strategy is to embed an entirely new smart-city traffic system, which can be done because convolutional neural networks do a great job of processing sensor and image-recognition data. To reiterate, this is already happening in US cities such Denver, Pittsburgh, and Phoenix. You're going to see a lot more of this technology in the next five to six years.

CHAPTER 14

CASE STUDY 4

DATA DEMOCRATIZATION VIA ROLE-BASED ACCESS AND BLOCKCHAIN

THE ASK STEPS
Ask

Asking great quesions that can be answered with data

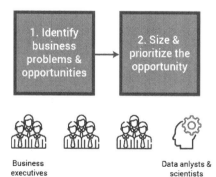

We live in an era of a wealth of data. Data is the gold or oil of the twenty-first century, and your data is your competitive advantage. You want to leverage it as much as possible, and you also need to protect and safeguard it as much as you can. One of the biggest issues in industry these days is how to provide the right data to the right people in an organization, in a smart, efficient, and also secure manner.

Data-driven decisions are better decisions, but organizations currently face three challenges in this respect:

1. **Systems:** Businesses don't have systems robust enough to efficiently handle the flood of data that flows into the enterprise. Therefore, they don't and can't provide the right people access to the data they need to enhance their decision-making and do their jobs most effectively. In other words, although data democratization is one of the fundamental principles of a data- and model-driven enterprise, most companies today don't know how to democratize data effectively.
2. **Regulatory and liability issues:** The complicating, paradoxical factor is that highly regulated industries, such as healthcare, banking, and insurance, can't fully democratize data within their own organization because of regulatory constraints and liability concerns.

3. **Data leakage:** If you democratize all data to everyone, you run the risk that it will become visible outside the organization, possibly to competitors and the public at large. Since data is your competitive advantage, you don't want this to happen. Data leakage can be extremely harmful and expensive.

So it is difficult for large organizations to figure out how to democratize their data efficiently and securely, as important as such data democratization is. This is the initial business problem in this case study: how can we provide access to the right data to the right people within the enterprise in a dynamic, smart, secure way? There is a powerful opportunity here to drive positive change.

One suggestion, originally made in Part 1, is to create a role-based system. Look at roles, identify the decisions people in those roles (personas) make on a daily basis, and then map the data you have onto those roles and decisions. You can then give individuals access to the data, or at least the metadata, they need based on the decisions they are required to make in their roles.

In most large organizations, data governance officers currently control access to data and data transactions. This team is comprised of employees who, like police or traffic officers, grant access to data and determine the criteria for granting such access. Given the employee salaries and other costs involved, this is an expensive solution. It's also inefficient because data governance often takes a long time. It's also a less inclusive solution because some departments, especially technical ones, get more access to data than non-technical teams, such as marketing or operations, even though everyone makes the same number of important decisions every day. This approach is not only less inclusive but fundamentally incorrect.

What's more, one department doesn't necessarily know what data other departments have. There's no data or even metadata transparency, which creates a lot of barriers to providing the right data to the right people at the right time.

How would you meet this challenge? How would you turn this business problem into a data problem? Please take a minute or so to think about how you could efficiently democratize data in your organization.

The problem will be more easily solved if broken into two phases or parts:

1. Creating a dynamic role-based system that will provide insight into what data we should provide to specific roles within the enterprise.
2. Doing so in a secure way, safely providing the right keys to the right data to the right decision-maker.

All of this must happen automatically and dynamically, in real time, without the intervention of data-governance officers.

Relevant questions to pose here, in the first step of the ask phase, are:

- Can you leverage specific roles in an organization to create and distribute role-based keys to unlock the data relevant to the decisions those roles need to make?
- Can you leverage the data you already have on employees and their actions to understand and classify the data they will need regular access to going forward?
- Is there a system or infrastructure that can securely and reliably provide role-based access keys to give the right roles the right data at the right time and also maintain a full record of the transactions and data linked to each of these keys?

If you can specify the decisions made by roles or personas in an organization, you can provide each role with digital keys that will unlock relevant data held within the network. This case study will guide us through solving the first part of the problem—the first two of the three questions just posed—by using machine-intelligence techniques, some of which we've seen in previous case studies.

This case will also introduce you to an infrastructure that can be used to create a solution to the second part of the problem and the third of the questions just posed: security. This infrastructure is known as blockchain.

Most people associate blockchain with cryptocurrencies such as Bitcoin, but its applications go far beyond this. Blockchain technology will change the world in the next three to ten years. What the internet and social media did for information, blockchain will do for trustworthy transactions.

Blockchain uses cryptography to ensure transactions are trustworthy, fully documented, and recorded. It is a decentralized system, like the internet itself, that employs no intermediaries but that can be accessed by anyone with the proper permissions or keys.

The blockchain infrastructure is a great solution to providing immediate, dynamic, secure, and well-recorded access to relevant data. The technology can be used as the foundation of a real-time, role-based system, identifying and distributing keys to data based on the daily decisions a role needs to make.

As no intermediaries are involved, the blockchain process is efficient, fast, and effective. If you have the right key, you immediately have access to data. There's no need to go through the additional steps of finding the person who controls or can provide the authorization to access necessary data and making a request. The blockchain system will keep thorough records of all an organization's data and the access that has been granted to it.

The second step in the ask phase is to see what the ROI opportunity is by doing a back-of-the-envelope calculation. Better, smarter, data-driven decisions can revolutionize your business. If a trustworthy technology governs this system, you can also reduce the risk of data leakage, regulatory disputes, and data or financial liability.

According to IBM, the market for making better business decisions by leveraging data and modeling techniques is $2 trillion.[20] More specifically, blockchain technology could help consumers save up to $16 billion in banking and insurance fees per year by eliminating middlemen.[21] Institutions will realize comparable savings. More access to data also means there will be more data to input into

---

20 Barb Darrow, "Through Machine Learning, IBM Braintrust Sees Better Days Ahead," *Fortune,* February 25, 2016, http://fortune.com/2016/02/25/ibm-sees-better-days-ahead/; Julie Bort, "The IT industry is launching new markets worth more than $2 trillion, IBM CEO says," *Business Insider,* February 25, 2016, https://www.businessinsider.com/ibm-ceo-pursues-a-new-2-trillion-market-2016-2.

21 Deborah Dawson, "Blockchain - More than Digital Currency," International Legal Technology Association, November 14, 2017, https://www.iltanet.org/blogs/deborah-dobson/2017/11/14/blockchain-more-than-digital-currency?ssopc=1; Telis Demos, "Bitcoin's Blockchain Technology Proves Itself in Wall Street Test," *Wall Street Journal,* April 7, 2016, https://www.wsj.com/articles/bitcoins-blockchain-technology-proves-itself-in-wall-street-test-1460021421.

and train machine-intelligence models: the more data, the better the results.

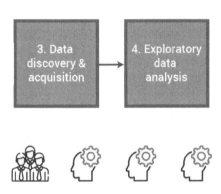

THE ACQUIRE STEPS

Acquire

Acquiring & preparing data for analysis

This acquire phase is about data discovery. There are two steps in the process you are embarking upon. First, build a role-based system that generates keys that allow employees immediate access to data that will enable them to enhance their decision-making process and do their jobs better. Then, implement the keys generated from and predicted by the machine learning models in a blockchain network so employees can access the right data immediately and securely.

Consider your marketing department. Marketers need to figure out what message will most resonate with a specific targeted audience. The content of those messages is based on specific profiles in the customer base, which cluster or classify people into groups.

In this case, the "role" is marketer, employees who need to decide what messages will resonate with different types of customers. Once this has been determined, the data a marketer needs to make such decisions can be identified. Each marketer will then have a key that can unlock this relevant marketing data at the right time through a trusted, secure blockchain network.

To create this kind of role-based system, you need to know what data the role needs regular access to. You must look at specific employee profiles and their interactions with current data files, social media data, CRMs, and the other systems they work with.

You also need macro-level departmental data: What do employees in a particular department do? Where are they positioned in the organizational hierarchy? What are the daily decisions they make? What data do they currently have? What additional data will help them make more data-driven decisions?

To build the system, you need to look at the requests these

employees send to your data-governance team, as well as their demographics. What data from outside their department do they regularly need? How much time does it now take them to acquire this data?

This exploratory data analysis (EDA) will give us insight into current inefficiencies and help you better understand how to break down the silos between different departments that contribute to inefficiency.

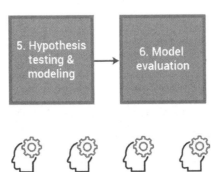

THE ANALYZE STEPS
Analyze
Applying modeling techniques to create predictive power

Now your technical team can focus on creating machine-intelligence models to predict and generate the keys on which the system is based. The goal is to generate keys that grant specific roles access to that data they need out of the entire universe of data input into the model, which can then be delivered through a secure blockchain infrastructure.

The underlying mechanism for using machine intelligence to generate keys is a model capable of understanding different underlying patterns in the data, categorizing roles, dynamically creating keys, and then iteratively measuring performance and usability to determine when keys and their properties need to be changed. This is known as dynamic model-setting. Keys and access change over time based on usage, new business initiatives, and the new outcomes and patterns the model generates.

In this case, two different models can be tested:

1. Matching algorithms, such as logistic regression, which can determine the probability that a key will match with a specific role.
2. Classification and clustering algorithms that will find data patterns capable of classifying or clustering different groups of unique roles based on the data they interact with daily. Appropriate keys can then be generated: roles are matched with keys giving access to the appropriate data.

Let's look at a concrete example. A marketing manager

at Google might receive keys 1, 3, 5, and 9, generated by one or more of the above machine-learning models. Key 1 provides access to data about different types of customers. Key 3 yields data on customers' preferred communication channels, such as email or social media. Key 5 gives access to different types of messages that might resonate with specific customer groups. Key 9 gives data on the time of day, such as when specific messages should be sent to specific groups.

The system identifies marketing tasks and generates keys that give access to the different types of data that will help marketers make better, data-driven decisions. These keys can change over time, based on observations of employee behavior and responsibilities.

An internal communications manager at Google might receive some of the same keys as a marketing manager, such as keys 3 and 5, as well as additional keys, such as keys 10 and 14. This role's assortment of keys is different from those assigned to any other role in the organization. The system then keeps running and validating the model, making it a dynamic learning cycle capable of changing keys and the data they can access over time, as circumstances change.

Evaluation then takes place, analyzing how the models are performing over time. The evaluation techniques employed are the same or similar to those covered in previous case studies.

A model is evaluated on whether it can provide the right people with the right data at the right time. How many mistakes does the model make? For example, if a barista in a hospital gets a patient's health record, an error has obviously been made. In doing an analysis of this kind, you want to look at both false positives and false negatives. The model's results can also be benchmarked and compared to the results of your organization's current, traditional data-governance process. Are the outcomes of the new process close to that of the old?

Act

Interpreting theoutcomes & operationalizing across the enterprise

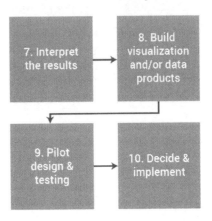

At the beginning of the act phase, you interpret the models' results and construct data visualizations. How can you be sure that a role will require access to the data unlocked by a specific key?

Interpreting results requires knowing the main predictors that generate keys. Such predictors might include which department someone works in, what their current access to data is, their job responsibilities, and their decision-making processes. If the models can identify these predictors and provide the relevant keys, the data-access process will be simplified and far more efficient because employees won't have to constantly ask data governance for permission to get the data they need.

Then ROI must be demonstrated. The risk of data leakage and misuse is lowered because of the blockchain architecture. The model will of course have to be trained over time and with time will perform better and better. Once the model is properly trained, there will be no data leakage or misuse due to the security the blockchain network provides. The business will have evolved, becoming more data- and model-driven, because now the right data can find the right people. Because these people can now make more and better data-driven decisions, the business will be revolutionized.

As mentioned in Part 1, leaders in the twenty-first century are expected to bring data and decisions closer together. The system just described can do this because people will get immediate access to data, based dynamically on the decisions they have to make on a daily basis. The system can also help habituate people to making data-driven decisions, better decisions.

Over time, the model will deliver ever-better results because it is being constantly enriched with relevant data generated by the ongoing use of the system. A positive feedback loop is created: more and better data will create better models, which will in turn generate better data. This will have a direct and significant impact on the organization's ROI.

Since a blockchain infrastructure records all transactions in a secure virtual ledger, you will now be able to recognize if, when, and why data leakage occurs. You will know exactly why the data was generated and who had access to it every step of the way. The blockchain's complete transaction history can enable you to discover mistakes and the reasons behind them so that they are not repeated.

The last step in the process is to make the decision to implement this system. As always, consider both your short-term and long-term strategies for role-based data-democratization. Please take a minute here to think about how you might tackle short-term implementation of such a system in your organization.

Once you identify roles and the daily decisions these roles make, you would pilot this machine-learning model in a small department. This will determine the accuracy of the keys generated and ensure that the blockchain architecture functions properly. The pilot will also enable you to test and validate the model's results. Once this has been done, you can begin implementing both role-based access and the blockchain infrastructure more widely.

In the long term, you will operationalize the system across the entire organization. This will involve more testing and validation of keys across different departments and roles to ensure the model triggers the right keys and that the blockchain infrastructure is able to provide fully secure access to the proper data.

CONCLUSION

The Fourth Industrial Revolution has already begun. Executives and business leaders now have the responsibility and opportunity of figuring out how to transform their organizations into data- and model-driven enterprises, the only way to ensure survival and growth in the coming years.

Looking at the machine-intelligence maturity curve described earlier, there are two phases to be explored: making your enterprise first data-driven, then model-driven. In the first phase, data is leveraged to make better business decisions: *all* business decisions. As your organization progresses along the maturity curve, it will start embedding machine-intelligence modeling techniques and automation in its daily operations. Advanced machine-intelligence techniques will give you the predictive power required to survive and thrive in the Fourth Industrial Revolution.

Start getting into the habit of imitating the tricks, tools, mindsets, and habits of a data- and model-driven enterprise. Start by taking small, intuitive actions. Above all, start by transforming yourself. Stop asking what you think. Start asking what you know: what does the data tell you?

Start changing your habits. Lead by example. Your direct reports will then start changing their habits, as will their direct reports and down the line. Your team looks up to you. Champion data and use a data-first approach when making business decisions. The data-and model-driven mindset will quickly amplify throughout the organization.

The biggest problem you face in the Fourth Industrial Revolution is not data or technology. It's people, culture, and process. These are where you'll find the barriers that prevent companies from fully embedding machine-intelligence technology. Everything starts with you and your people.

Look at yourself and how you behave. Look at your people and how you are leading and rallying them around this game-changing technology. Look at the change management required to create an infrastructure that can both handle an ever-increasing flood of data and generate the best responses to the predictions that sophisticated machine-intelligence models make.

Remember the six principles of a data-driven organization given in Chapter 4:

1. Data strategy
2. Data democratization, which is one of the biggest gaps organizations are currently experiencing
3. A data- and model-driven culture
4. "Speed to insight": how to derive insights from your data as quickly as possible
5. Data science value as a key performance indicator (KPI)
6. Data governance, security, and privacy

These principles are not a recipe, a measured number of action steps that will move you from x to y. They're guiding principles, ideas you can borrow and learn from, just as you can learn from the examples of how other companies went through this transformation and are already thriving in the Fourth Industrial Revolution.

Take these principles and make them your own. They are part of your new landscape. Go back to your organization and figure out how you can personalize these six principles in terms of your organization's people, mission, technology, infrastructure, and ecosystem.

Again, stop blaming the data, because you already have a lot of data, and stop blaming the technology, because there are many technology infrastructure providers that can support you. There's a big open-source community that can help meet your technology needs and challenges if that's what you require.

The true problem is execution, processes, change management, and your behavior. It's the *people*. And who are the people at the root of the problem? Not to mince words, it's executives: business leaders, functional leaders, regional leaders, and general managers.

Most business leaders don't understand the machine-intelligence space or how to create an environment where data scientists and your technical team can work together seamlessly with your business team so that all parties thrive. Data science and machine intelligence are top-down initiatives.

Trying to make these changes from the bottom up is a recipe for failure. Changes in business processes must come from the top. They must come from the CEO, who should champion data and create a culture in which data scientists and the technical team can succeed and thrive.

Create links between technical and non-technical people and fund educational programs that will reskill, upskill, and create new skills among current employees, enabling your company to leverage this technology and these techniques to harness data to increase the services you provide to your clients, customers, or users. This will push and grow your organization.

You must adopt a data-science mindset, which is why a focus of this book has been to guide you through the data-science workflow, both in the abstract and with concrete case studies. You don't have to become a data scientist, but you do have to develop the critical thinking that will enable you to evaluate machine-learning technology, models, and outcomes quickly and intelligently. If you develop such critical thinking, you'll be able both to critique results and create a machine-intelligence strategy. You'll be able to think about how to leverage the data you have to create greater modeling and forecasting power for your organization.

Always celebrate wins! Once you embark on this journey and generate ROI, showcase your accomplishments. CEOs often tell me, "We ran an education program. Our employees created amazing projects that were embedded in our system, but we never celebrated them. Other departments don't know about them."

Don't let this happen to you. Celebrate wins. Word of mouth is important because it helps cross-pollinate. If one department successfully creates and implements a model, showcase it as a case study to the entire organization.

CALL TO ACTION

Start now. It's already late in the game, but I believe large organizations are able to transform themselves. Short-term changes can be made quickly. Figure out the change management required and the cultural and funding aspects involved. These are all vital steps to boot-strapping your organization into the Fourth Industrial Revolution. Companies that harness data with advanced modeling techniques will be able to fight and win in this fast-paced, competitive, exponentially growing and changing landscape.

If you're just starting, start small. When you start small within different departments, you create a hub-and-spoke infrastructure eventually capable of changing the entire organization. People will start thinking differently and adopting the right mindset. They will begin getting their data into the right shape and understanding how to translate their business problems into data problems. Slowly but surely, they will get into the habit of solving business problems with data and modeling techniques—even if they don't know and never intend to learn how to code.

Calculate the ROI of your first machine-intelligence solution. Then, when it makes sense from a business standpoint, expand and reinvest. After realizing ROI from pilot projects, start investing in more initiatives and figure out how you can leverage one project horizontally into other departments in your organization.

GET STARTED

At this point, you should realize that probably all your top five business problems can be solved by leveraging data and modeling techniques. Let's go through a brief interactive process that will help you get started on applying what you have learned in this book to your own business.

One of the goals of this book is to enable you to start the journey and begin thinking about your data strategy. Go to this book's Appendix A and write down your top five business problems. Choose one and begin the ten-step workflow that will enable you to come up with data-driven, machine-intelligence solutions.

What are some interesting questions you might pose about this issue that would start turning it from a business problem into a data problem? Once you identify a use case, start measuring it from a priority perspective. Does it demonstrate high impact and high feasibility? Do a quick back-of-the-envelope calculation of the ROI a solution to this problem could generate. If you think the project would have a significant impact, keep going. If not, turn to another one of your top business problems.

You can start now start thinking about and writing down the data you would need to collect to solve the problem. Remembering that there is no one winning horse at this point in the game, do you have a sense of what machine-intelligence techniques might be tested and applied to this data? If you're stumped—or even if you're not—talk this over with your technical team. As you continue through the process, write down your answers and discoveries in the appendix.

Machine-intelligence projects are the future of business innovation, and innovation is what drives monetization. What new machine-intelligence-based products and services could you create to attract revenue and grow your business? Bring them to the table and get started on this fascinating journey.

FILLING THE GAPS

The first issue that arises in any machine-intelligence gap analysis is people. Another major, related gap is the current lack of awareness and education. Both issues relate to management, leadership, culture, funding, and an understanding of the machine-intelligence space. This book was written to give business leaders such as yourself basic training in this essential subject.

Another big barrier is bringing technical and non-technical teams together. From an operations perspective, executives, business teams, and technical teams all have a lot of shared responsibility in the Fourth Industrial Revolution. In the past, enterprises never involved technical teams in decision-making and change management. Only executives and business people made such decisions. Now, engineers and data scientists must also participate.

Business leaders must learn how to work with their technical teams to effectively embed them into change-management processes. If the gap between business and technical teams is not bridged, your organization won't be able to implement and realize the ROI from machine-intelligence projects.

The third and last big necessary cultural change is to start thinking about change management at the very beginning of machine-intelligence initiatives, not at the end. If you don't do this, you won't be able to realize potential ROI and will simply waste a lot of money.

The good news is that business leaders are fully capable of both making and leading such changes. I experience the truth of this with every enterprise I work with.

We are living in an era of Human + Machine. The technology is here to augment and extend your intelligence. It is not trying to replace you or make decisions on your behalf. Simply put, it's a "brain helper" in an era of a wealth of data and unbounded opportunity. Embrace this technology, as it can complement you and help push your organization to the next level. Data will enable you to learn, and better, cleaner, and more reliable data will help you to learn exponentially. Data is critical, and its care and cultivation are ultimately your responsibility.

LOOKING FORWARD

Microsoft CEO Satya Nadella once said, "We are pursuing AI so that we can empower every person and every institution that people build with tools of AI so that they can go on to solve the most pressing problems of our society and our economy."

If you start at the top—if you establish the right culture and augment the power of the technology—the message will amplify throughout the entire organization.

Maybe your organization will solve a crucial problem, whether it's cancer or another disease, warfare, economic crisis, hunger, or homelessness. There are many ways that you might reshape society, leveraging machine-intelligence techniques, to make the world a better, safer place for the next generation. It may not be simple or easy journey, but it is possible.

The current skills gap in the use of machine intelligence in the industry is enormous.[22] But over and above the skills gap, we need to acknowledge that the Fourth Industrial Revolution will change every one of our jobs in the near future. To make this revolution work for the benefit of our economy and society, we need to be inclusive: everyone in the workforce can and must be able to participate, not just people with the "right" degrees or credentials. Technology will always continue to change over time, and we are going to have to continue to reskill and invent new skills so that no one is left behind.

While this technology provides opportunities, it also introduces big new challenges. Trust and transparency must be at its core. Working with leaders at large technology enterprises—the ones that create the chips and infrastructure that enable us to deploy machine-intelligence models—I learned that technology development is based on the following guiding principles:

1. **Purpose:** The technology's purpose is to augment our intelligence and help us do what we do, not to replace us.
2. **Trust:** Your data belongs to your organization, is your competitive advantage, and must be fully protected.

---

22 LinkedIn Economic Graph Team, "LinkedIn Workforce Report | United States | August 2018," August 2018, https://economicgraph.linkedin.com/resources/linkedin-workforce-report-august-2018.

3. **Transparency:** Data scientists and other technologists must do all we can to explain and help you to understand how these sophisticated models generate predictions, shedding light on questions such as how these models are trained and what data was input into them to generate their output and predictions.

The message is very consistent among all major players in the field. We must embrace this technology, trust it, and employ it to our benefit.

The speed of change and technological advancements has never been seen before in any other industrial revolution. The world is more complex and volatile today than any other time in our history. We must understand and acknowledge the fact that artificial intelligence is no longer a future fantasy or a chapter in a computer-science textbook. We are at a crucial point in history when everyone should know and understand how to enable, deploy, and implement this technology to solve the fundamental economic, social, and environmental issues we are now facing.

Please do not hesitate to reach out to me at ds4e@nirkaldero.com with any question or for any guidance you seek for your professional or organizational growth.

I hope this book has ignited your ambition to lead profound change through data in your organization and the world around you.

APPENDIX A

YOUR DATA-STRATEGY FRAMEWORK WORKSHEET

DATA

Data is the raw material for the insight and foresight necessary for decision-making. Data can become a competitive differentiator.

- Target/Goal (describe):

- Current State (how do things currently look?):

- Future State (what should they look like?):

- Next Steps (that you can take/make):

1.

2.

CULTURE

Culture is set by leadership; data science simultaneously involves people, technology, and data assets.

- Target/Goal:

- Current State:

- Future State:

- Next Steps:

1.

2.

TALENT

The right skillset is crucial to unlocking data science opportunities.

- Target/Goal:

- Current State:

- Future State:

- Next Steps:
1.

2.

TECH

The right technological infrastructure enables you to digest, process, and visualize data in order to make better and more efficient decisions.

- Target/Goal:

- Current State:

- Future State:

- Next Steps:

1.

2.

APPLYING DATA-SCIENCE WORKFLOW TO YOUR BUSINESS PROBLEMS

Write down your top five business problems:

1.

2.

3.

4.

5.

What data will be required to solve each of these business problems?

1.

2.

3.

4.

5.

Which two business problems demonstrate the highest impact and feasibility? These are the ones you should focus on.

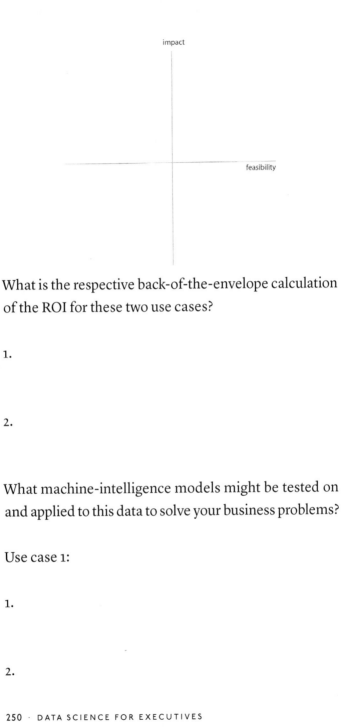

What is the respective back-of-the-envelope calculation of the ROI for these two use cases?

1.

2.

What machine-intelligence models might be tested on and applied to this data to solve your business problems?

Use case 1:

1.

2.

Use case 2:

1.

2.

What are the change-management and operational processes required for the implementation of the machine-intelligence solutions?

Use case 1:

1.

2.

Use case 2:

1.

2.

What are your short- and long-term implementation strategies?

Use case 1:

1.

2.

Use case 2:

1.

2.

APPENDIX B

THE THREE MAIN TYPES OF MACHINE-LEARNING ALGORITHMS

To leverage machine learning to benefit your organization, you don't have to grasp theoretical details. However, you do need to have a high-level understanding of some technical terminology. There are three main types of machine-learning algorithms: **supervised learning algorithms, unsupervised learning algorithms,** and **semi-supervised learning algorithms.** We'll look at them one by one.

Supervised learning involves prior knowledge of both sample input (x) and what the output values (y) resulting from the processing of that input should be. Supervised learning's goal is to come up with a mathematical function that best approximates the generalized relationship between input and output observable in this sample data, which is also known as training data. **Unsupervised learning**, on the other hand, does not have labeled input, so its goal is to determine the underlying structure of and trends within a set of data points. **Semi-supervised learning** is a hybrid version of the two.

SUPERVISED LEARNING ALGORITHMS

Most practical machine learning today involves supervised learning. With supervised learning, input variables (x) and an output variables (y) are used to derive or determine the function (f) that describes how the input links or maps to the output:

$$y = f(x)$$

Supervised learning algorithms learn from historical, observed data or facts. These serve as the basis or "ground truth" on which a predictive analysis can be made.

The goal of supervised learning is to best approximate the mapping function so that when new data (x) is input, the model will be able to predict the resulting output variables (y). The process by which such a model learns from a data set is similar to that of an educator supervising a learning process: therefore, the name "supervised learning." Since we know the correct answers or output in the original training data, the algorithm iteratively makes predictions based on additional training input, and is corrected as needed. This learning process ends when the algorithm achieves an acceptable pre-determined level of performance.

Think of x as an input and y as an output of a model that attempts to answer the question "What is the likelihood a potential customer will decide to buy an iPhone instead of an Android?" Input x includes all known data and features, like size, color, and user preferences. Output y is the pre-defined target, whether you bought an iPhone or not. Once output, y then iteratively becomes part of input x, improving the algorithm's ability to make correct predictions by refining the direct mapping function between x and y.

Supervised learning algorithms utilize a few principal techniques in creating predictive models. The first is **regression**. In regression, the output or target variable is a real value, such as "dollars" or "weight." Consider house pricing. A regression analysis will help predict the price of a house based on historical data on local and national housing markets. It predicts a specific house's price (y) by minimizing the distance between observed data and the predicted value, more and more closely approximating the price by mapping input to output.

Trulia is a great example of this. It predicts house prices

extremely accurately using regression analysis on market data. Stock-price prediction engines also use supervised learning algorithms based on regression techniques.

Classification is another supervised learning algorithm technique. The output variable (y) of a classification problem is a category, such as "blue," "green," or "spam/not spam." Classification assigns new data to the class to which it most likely belongs, based on a classification model built from labeled training data.

Great examples of classification are machine-learning algorithms that determine whether email can be classified as spam or not, or whether a loan application is fraudulent. The data used to classify emails as spam contains a lot of features, such as the size of the email, word count, recipient, sender, and so on. These features are gathered from previous emails that have been identified as either spam or not spam. The target output y is an answer to the question "Is this email spam or not?"

When a new email comes in, the algorithm attempts to determine whether it is spam. A classification algorithm calculates the probability that the email is spam. With these probabilities in mind, a threshold is set, above which the model identifies an email as spam, and below which it does not.

UNSUPERVISED LEARNING ALGORITHMS

Supervised learning algorithms learn from observed facts. In unsupervised learning algorithms, only input data (x) is known while corresponding output variables (y) are unknown. Unsupervised learning's goal is to discover and model underlying structures or patterns in the data.

These are called unsupervised learning algorithms because, unlike supervised learning, there are no previously known correct answers or output, and therefore no "educator" supervising the learning. The algorithms are left to their own devices to discover and present interesting structures in the data, which are relevant to the specific problem to be solved.

Unsupervised learning can be further grouped into **clustering** and **association** problems. **Clustering** is one of the most popular unsupervised learning techniques. A clustering problem is one in which inherent or underlying groupings in the data—such as grouping customers by purchasing behavior—need to be identified and predicted. The goal of clustering is to create groups of data points in which points in different clusters are dissimilar while points within each of these different clusters are similar.

Think about a corporate marketing division that wants to cluster customers into groups so it can provide each group with specifically tailored messages. There is no pre-identified output data determining what the groups are and which customers belong to which groups. The clustering algorithm takes all the data and information that already exists and then finds patterns in the data that sorts customers into different buckets according to parameters the algorithm itself determines.

Clustering gathers groups of customers together based on different methods, such as **k-means clustering**, which clusters data points into k number of groups. A larger k creates smaller groups with more granularity; a smaller k yields larger groups and less granularity. Another method is **hierarchical clustering**, which is similar to k-means clustering, except that the technique creates a hierarchy of clusters. For example, think about grouping items on an online marketplace such as Amazon. To simplify navigation, the homepage presents only a few broad categories or groups of items. As the user navigates into more specific shopping categories, the level of granularity increases. In subpages, new clusters of items represent a different level of the clustering hierarchy.

Association is another unsupervised technique, used specifically to determine similarities within data patterns. Recommendation engines often use association to find commonalities in user preferences and actions.

Association does not deal with observed or labeled data

but finds patterns of commonality or association within unlabeled data, which then enable recommendations to be made. A good example is Facebook making recommendations based not on your own interests but on the interests of your Facebook friends.

Association algorithms filter data using a few different approaches. One is **content-based**, in which a recommended product has attributes similar to other products you like or have purchased. To take another Facebook example, if you click, comment on, or otherwise interact with content on your Facebook page, the algorithm will find and recommend similar content.

Association algorithms' second and most popular approach is **collaborative filtering**. The algorithm looks at other users who have "liked" the same products or news articles you have viewed and then recommends the products those users have "liked" or purchased to you. There are now two customers: me and you. I've read some articles on Facebook, you've read other articles, and we're "friends." The algorithm will find these patterns and provide us each with more content or products based on how the other one behaved.

To summarize, in the content-based approach, the user has interacted with content, and, based on that content, Facebook recommends new content. In the collaborative-filtering approach, there are two users who interact and share, and Facebook recommends content based on these shared behaviors, having learned the similarities between two or more different users.

At this point, a clustering algorithm that recommends products that go well together can be plugged in. All three subcategories of unsupervised learning algorithms—content-based association, collaborative-filtering association, and clustering—work together to build particularly strong recommendation engines that exponentially increase potential purchases.

SEMI-SUPERVISED LEARNING ALGORITHMS

Semi-supervised learning problems involve a large amount of input data (x), only some of which is labeled. These problems sit between supervised and unsupervised learning.

A good example is a photo archive in which only some images are labeled (e.g. dog, cat, person) and the majority is unlabeled. Many real-world machine-learning problems, such as those involving voice, image, or sensor data, fall into this category. It can be expensive and time-consuming to label data, and such labeling may need to be done by domain experts. One the other hand, unlabeled data is cheap and easy to collect and store.

Keeping this data unstructured is more efficient at the beginning of the process but can be costly afterward because you need a lot of computational power to find the patterns in such large data sets. A lot of feature engineering is also required to give numeric values to non-numeric sound and image data.

Semi-supervised learning can make best-guess predictions for unlabeled data using unsupervised learning techniques. These can then be used as training data in a supervised learning model, which in turn can make predictions based on data subsequently input.

"Deep learning" neural networks, one of the principal cutting-edge semi-supervised learning algorithm models, try to imitate the flow of information in our brains. There's an input layer, an output layer, and many other layers in between. In the real world, information or data also travels through the different layers of neurons in our brains in a non-linear fashion, in which everything is connected to everything. Neural-network semi-supervised learning algorithms discern deep patterns and interesting resources in this type of inter-connected, non-linear flow of unstructured, unlabeled data. Doing so, however, is quite expensive computationally.

Often, the applications of semi-supervised learning algorithms, because they deal with real-world input, seem quite ordinary. Handwriting, for example, is unstructured data. When we try to understand a doctor's handwriting on a prescription, the machine first applies image-recognition, then natural-language processing to "read" the text.

There are similar human resources (HR) applications. The resumes you may want to screen are not numeric but are unstructured images, like PDF files. Deep-learning models are frequently applied by HR departments to find the best candidate for a position based on visual and audio files.

Facebook and the military have done a lot of work on facial recognition that involves semi-supervised learning algorithms working with unstructured visual data. They aren't alone. Consider the facial-recognition feature of the iPhone X, which allows you to unlock your iPhone simply by looking at it. That's a "deep-learning" unsupervised learning technique: there's a large neural network behind the model, which captures your face as input, analyzes it in the "in-between layers" and determines, as output, whether you are you or not. Training the system to do this takes some time, but eventually it recognizes your face efficiently, and unlocks your phone. As will be discussed below, training neural networks takes time—think of the OODA loop—but they continue to learn as they receive additional input.

ABOUT THE AUTHOR

From his time in the Israeli Defense Force to overseeing data science at a leading education company, Nir Kaldero's profound understanding of data science has made him one of the world's foremost trainers to high-impact executives in how to transform their organizations into robust, data- and model-driven corporations.

In addition to his work at some of the world's largest international corporations, Kaldero created a graduate program in data science and serves as a Google expert/mentor and IBM Champion. Winner of countless STEM awards, Kaldero's insights are in high demand around the globe. He can be contacted at www.ds4e@nirkaldero.com.

WOULD YOUR TEAM BENEFIT FROM READING
DATA SCIENCE FOR EXECUTIVES?

With our Enterprise pricing, you can
save up to 20% off the book's price when
ordering copies for your team.

For more information, visit www.DS4E.com/

Made in the USA
Middletown, DE
27 October 2020